# "DICKS OUT!"

**The definitive work on British football songs**

by

**Larry Bulmer**

and

**Rob Merrills**

A proportion of the proceeds of this book will be divided between two charities; the Football Against Multiple Sclerosis appeal, and the Tunbridge Wells Seven Springs Cheshire Home, which takes disabled residents to Football League matches on a regular basis. Thank you for your support.

Written and Edited by:
Larry Bulmer & Rob Merrills

Illustrations by:
Bill Beacham

© Chatsby Publishing

Second Impression 1992

Published in Great Britan by
Chatsby Publishing
P O Box 252
Tunbridge Wells
Kent   TN2 3XL
England

Printed by D C Graphics,
Bexhill-on-Sea, East Sussex

Paper supplied by Fenner Paper,
Tonbridge, Kent

Bound by Kensett Bookbinders,
Brighton, East Sussex

British Library Cataloguing in Publication Data

Bulmer, Larry. 1963 -
Merrills, Rob. 1965 -
Dicks Out! - 2nd imp.
1. Association Football
I. Title II. Bulmer, Larry &
Merrills, Rob
xxxxxxxxxxx
xxxxxxxxxxx

ISBN 1 874546 00 2

To Linda

*"She makes my day(s)!"*


To Ann

*T M W W A*

and Dad,

to return the compliment


and not forgetting Neil and Dave

without who's efforts on the tea making

front, this colossus of 1990's

literary work may never have happened.

# CONTENTS

# INTRODUCTION

When this book was conceived - way back in 1989 - all was (reasonably) well with our National Game. Since then we have witnessed the rise to power of those who would basically be happy to throw away over a century of tradition and replace it with the passionless, money motivated Premier League. Not only will this profit obsessed monster devour a number of the League's smaller clubs, it's creation has sounded the death knell for the terraces on which the songs contained herein are currently performed. Whilst an independent Football League may have stood up to UEFA over the implementation of the all encompassing and farcical all seater directive, the Premier League officials have grasped the suggested regulation with both hands, as it gives them all the power they need to consign the Kippax's and Shelf's of this world to oblivion (or in the case of some lower divison club's, the grounds themwelves may disappear). Unwittingly, then, this book may have taken on the roll of an epitaph to the terraces, and to the humour, cameraderie and atmosphere which was always apparent amongst those who chose to stand there.

The parasites who seek to turn the Beautiful Game into a money making circus, beholden to the great god Television, would be more than happy to see the fans who make up the singing choirs throughout the League priced out of the game entirely, to be replaced with monied businessmen who have no feeling for the game but who are more than happy to part with vast sums of money in the cause of corporate entertainment. It has always been a case of "them and us", with a few soundproofed executive boxes providing a safe haven where multi million pound deals can be clinched whilst the incumbents are insulated and oblivious from the passion play being enacted below them. It now looks as if things will turn full circle, with the few who wish to "get involved" with the game, and who can still afford to get in, will be in the minority and will have to be catered for by way of small enclosures in what will otherwise be glorified hospitality lounges. The songs and chants which have been a traditional part of our game for so long will inevitably fade into obscurity, and the game will undeniably be the poorer for their passing. Whilst we can still hope that this apocalyptic projection of the future may yet be avoided, it would seem that the first steps have already been taken in the emasculation of the game we love. This publication has, therefore, set out to catalogue as many of the games' songs as possible before they are forgotten (and also to put right ill informed commentators and journalists who occasionaly attempt to "inform" us about song derivations and usage).

The material for our effort was compiled over three years, by writing to a wide selection of fanzines, from which we received an excellent response and all of whom are credited in our "Acknowledgements" section. Every club's programme editor was also targetted for an approach, and a good many of them consented to print our appeals for information in their particular organs. In spite of the diligence of our quest for knowledge, there were a few clubs' supporters who were unwilling to impart details of their repertoires to us, no matter how vigorously we persued them, and they will therefore find their club's sadly missing from our scribblings. If anyone out there is able to contribute anything worthwhile for any such omitted club then please feel free to do so. Equally, if any of the information we have printed is incorrect - either the roots of songs or their words - then again, please let us know. Should the volume of this new information be large enough, we shall endeavour to produce a revised and updated volume in the future. With regard to the accuracy or otherwise of words, we have in many cases no personal knowledge of the songs we have catalogued and have therefore had to take what we receive as gospel. In some instances (notably in the Scottish section) we received conflicting versions of the same song, and here we have tried to pick out the most coherent format to print. The allocation of the names of tunes has also proved to be rather contentious in some cases - where a tune was not disclosed by our contributors we have either admitted our ignorance(!) or put in a tune which seemed to fit the lyrics in a rather pleasing manner (again, we stand to be corrected if you know we've got something wrong).

With the text which accompanies the songs, we have tried to give as much background information as possible, about both the songs themselves and the supporters who sing them. In spite of many a vain attempt at editorial discretion, personal bias has come through in a number of instances, so we apologise unreservedly to the supporters of any clubs who feel they may have come in for an unduely hard time. Inevitably, some of the songs are directed at individuals (more particularly the abusive ones!) and we would point out that the opinions voiced in such ditties are most definately not our own. We did, however, feel obliged to include such songs in order to give an accurate reflection of the feelings prevalent on the terraces at certain clubs. We did, though, make a conscious descision to exclude anything which referred to any sensitive episode from a clubs past in a derogatory manner (ie Munich, Hillsborough, the death of a well known figure etc). This sort of song does not deserve to be preserved in any way, least of all in a book which in no small way endeavours to put over the wit of the terrace songsters.

Anyway, that's just about enough introductory drivel from us - high time to let the supporters and songs of British football take centre stage......

Larry Bulmer & Rob Merrills
March 1992

# Section One

# The South East

1) **Brighton and Hove Albion**

2) **Gillingham**

3) **Maidstone United**

4) **Portsmouth**

5) **Reading**

6) **Southend United**

7) **Southampton**

# THE SOUTH EAST

The Garden of England, Sussex and Hampshire have never been regarded as being a great bastion of footballing passion, and the selection of songs we received from the southern clubs has done nothing to dispel this idea. All the clubs in the region are perhaps better known for cup exploits rather than any sustained spell of league success which is perhaps neccessary for the development of a cross section of songs and chants (apart, that is, from Portsmouth's "glory days" just after the war, which pre-dated the era of football songs). Southampton, in particular, have made the most of their trips to Wembley with several compostions centred around appearances in the shadow of the Twin Towers.

Pompey, in recent times, have lead very much of an up and down existaence with regard to league football - any enthusiasm generated by their brief flirtations with the higher divisions being tempered by a number of seasons in the twilight zones of the Third and Fourth. The level of support for the clubs seems to be very variable, with a large number of casual fans willing to make an appearance only for big Cup games - this, too, is not particularly helpful in the development of a good singing repertoire.

The lesser lights of the region have a catalogue of devotional hymnals comensurate with their lowly standing and general lack of success, although Reading and Maidstone United have quite a selection of the more eccentric chants often found in the lower divisions (even if the bulk of the latters' material dates from their not too distant non-league days).

Attendances in the south east seem to be very poor when the high density of population is taken in to account - some of the bigger clubs from elsewhere in the country can seemingly lay claim to having more support throughout the area than can the local clubs. This marked dilution of support can, again, only have a detrimental effect on the nature of the teams' followings and the passion of the vocal support.

Few, if any, popular chants have developed in the south which have subsequently spread northwards - with a couple of notable exceptions both having sprung from the Goldstone Ground. Firstly, as detailed in the club section, we have the "Peter Ward" effort which has given rise to so many derivatives since its inception and then, as briefly mentioned, they claim to have started the "Celery" chant which went on to notoriety at Stamford Bridge. This is very much an uncoroborated assertion on our part, with the tales of the Caveman Crew only coming from one source (cheers, Jason!), so , yet again, if anyone can shed any more light on the matter, we would be glad to hear from you.

# BRIGHTON AND HOVE ALBION

Disco's, white shoes, and ex-managers on the terraces are the few subjects for which Brighton F C is known, the town being more famous for a misplaced architectural wonder which would be better suited to Eden Gardens, Calcutta. The sadly misguided few who choose to follow the Albion have done little to earn the town any notoriety for the volume of its club's vocal support - only really laying claim to one fairly well known song, as detailed later. For the most part, the terraces of the Goldstone Ground would appear to be one of the quieter outposts of League football - even since the reappearance of the roof over the North Bank in the late 1980's. We may be doing the supporters a gross disservice, as there is probably a local bylaw prohibiting any form of voluble chanting in a public place for fear of bringing on coronaries or panic attacks amongst the large local population of geriatrics, who, in their formative years may have been responsible for the earliest substantiated performance of a football song we have yet come across. Cast your minds back (?) to those heady days of 1931 and a fearsome F A Cup clash between Brighton then of the Third Division (South) and Leicester City of the First Division. The foundations of the ground shook with a particularly strident rendition of *"Who Killed Cock Robin?"* - which was an allusion to the Leicestershire Constabulary who were known to all and sundry as "Redbreasts".

Back even further into the dim mists of time we find the origins of Brighton's most enduring song, *"(Good Old) Sussex by the Sea"*. This was apparently sung by the soldiers of the Sussex Regiment whilst carrying out training manoeuvres at the Goldstone Ground prior to fighting for King and Country in the trenches of Flanders. It has since been adopted by both the supporters, and the club as its official signature tune.....

> "Good old Sussex by the sea,
> Good old Sussex by the sea,
> For we're going up,
> And we'll win the Cup,
> For Sussex by the sea".

This song's most vociferous performances have been reserved for Brighton's ill fated appearances at Wembley, both for the '83 Cup Final(s) and the '91 play off fixture - the latter seeing an interesting struggle for vocal supremacy with Notts County's *"Wheelbarrow Song"* - the aptly nicknamed Magpies winning both this contest and a place in the First Division. The misery of the Seagull's contingent was compounded by the fact that this game also saw the debut of the infamous clownlike red and white away kit.

Apart from this, Brighton's players are rarely serenaded with any songs other than the succinct, if less than complex, chant of *"Seagulls...Seagulls"*. Even this simplistic effort was plagiarised from another club - the *"Eagles...Eagles"* drone from Selhurst Park being the inspiration. The rivalry between these two clubs also gave rise to the occasional assertion by Brighton's followers that any especially woeful opposition they encounter are *"Worse than Crystal Palace"* - even though it is highly unlikely that any team, no matter how bad, can genuinely be considered this incompetent. One last truly seminal piece from the South Coast is from the period 1975-80 (and later) when the prolific Peter Ward was feted with....

"He shot, he scored, he must be Peter Ward, Peter Ward".

Though not strictly speaking a song, the rhythmic structure has engendered an infinite number of variants, such as...

"He shot, he missed, he must be f**king pissed"
(Insert name of relevant player - twice)

"He's here, he's there, he's every f**king where,
Brian McClair, Brian McClair"

....and

"He's fat, he's round,  He bounces on the ground,
Sammy Lee, Sammy Lee".
(or any other obese person who deserves abuse)

Rumour has it that Brighton were also the originators of the "Celery" chant which has since been adopted by Chelsea. Apparently, this took off in the mid eighties as the theme tune of the Caveman Crew who initiated new members by way of some unseemly practices involving the said vegetable and a suitable bodily orifice whilst on the town's pier. Finally, a superb piece of opportunism as displayed by a very small section (ie the two authors of this book and an extremely attractive third party) of the visiting Crawley Town support during the 3rd round F A Cup tie at the Goldstone in January '92. Inspired by Brighton's truly hideous playing kit (the traditional blue and white stripes having continued off the bottom of the shirts down across the shorts) the crisp winter afternoon was rudely interrupted by an impromtu performance of the theme tune to *"Andy Pandy"* - *"Goodbye, goodbye, Andy and Teddy are waving goodbye. Time to go home, time to go home..."* etc. At the very least, this means that we can now write with some authority on which songs are a complete load of rubbish, having been solely responsible for this farcical interlude ourselves!

# GILLINGHAM

One of Kent's footballing outposts, the Priestfield Stadium does not appear to be a hotbed of terrace songs. Having achieved nothing of any great note, apart from relegating Sunderland and bringing the barter system of trading back into football by grossly overrating a certain forward of Italian origin and deeming him to have the equivalent fiscal worth of a set of tracksuits. Mind you a tidy profit was made which would have certainly cheered a certain thinning T.V commentator. Seeming to be scared of the second division, Gillingham spent a few seasons - with a reasonable team - missing promotion by various different, but always extremely close, margins. The expected glut of songs which could have immortalised these nearly-men did not materialize, or if they did then no-one told us, anything else out there all you Gills fans? They did, however, take the trouble to write in with a couple of "thug" songs from the early seventies, yes, even the Medway Towns had their fair share of itinerant hooligans, witness the following......

> "We ain't Jack and Jill,
> We ain't Bill and Ben,
> We ain't Ken Dodd or his Diddy men,
> We ain't Looby Loo with all her toys,
> We are the Gillingham BOOT BOYS,
> (Tune: *"Just one of those songs"* )

Along the same dated lines, and perhaps an early celebration of the balding features of a yet to be appointed Vice-President.....

> "Walking down the High Street swinging my chain,
> Along came a copper and he asked my name,
> So I kicked him in the Bo****ks,
> Stabbed him in the head,
> We are the Gillingham skinheads!"
> (Tune: Common Chant)

Both the above songs were performed by a large group of skinheads, who are now all married with children. According to our correspondent, recalling that he was once party to this sort of stuff causes acute embarrasment and reduces him to hysterics. We trust that Gillingham devotees no longer peddle this violence inducing rubbish. Certainly the gentleman (!) who recalls these sings them no more, having emigrated to Australia. Probably the best place for a Gills fan.

# MAIDSTONE UNITED

The Stones' vocal following has taken a turn for the worse since their promotion to the Football League, as have their fortunes in general. In common with many lower division clubs, their most hated rivals at present are not those who provide a source of long standing enmity through local derbies, but are the Local Authorities responsible for enforcing the Taylor Reports recommendations or, in the Stones' case, who are doing their utmost to force the club out of business by refusing planning application for a new ground. Their enforced exile at Dartford and the pathetic machinations of the Council bureaucrats provided the inspriation for this effort (a variation on the seminal Den effort)......

> "We are Maidstone, we are Maidstone,
> Super Maidstone, from nowhere,
> We are Maidstone, we are Maidstone,
> Super Maidstone, from nowhere,
> No one likes us, no one likes us,
> The Council hate us, we don't care,
> We are Maidstone, from nowhere".
> (Tune: *"Sailing"* by Rod Stewart).

With results being generally less than impressive, and the sparse surroundings of Watling Street hardly being conducive to producing a good atmosphere, the Football League has yet to see the best of the Stones supporters on the singing front. However, looking back to the not too distant past and the succesful days in the (then) Alliance Premier league, we find a time when the covered terrace at London Road was the venue for much stupidity. This was aptly illustrated during a six goal thrashing of Trowbridge Town - an evening match with a full moon rising majestically in the night sky. With events on the pitch being too one sided to provide much entertainment, the moon found itself the centre of attention, being serenaded with "Are you really made of cheese?", and the scientifically correct assertion that "You're a f**king long way away".

The astronomical idiocy escalated, with "We get pissed and ride on spaceships, la, la, la, la, la, la, la, la, la", and "If you're all going to Venus, clap your hands". This strange school of thought remained popular for some time, many people at non league grounds up and down the country being completely bemused by the "We are the Maidstone Moon Boys" chant. On a more down to earth note, the player responsible for much of the club's success through his prodigious goal scoring feats was often feted with....

"I'm dreaming of a Frank Ovard,
 Just like the one in every game,
 When the ball come over,
 Frank fell over,
 And the ref cried "Penalty!" again".
 (Tune: *"White Christmas"* )

While not specifically referring to the inordinate number of goals Frank scored, this song celebrates his ability to win penalties on an extremely regular basis, usually (to quote our contributor) "By taking a dive so obvious that Stevie Wonder would have seen it!" Still in the non league days, before Gillingham had assumed the mantle of despised local rivals, there was this brief but expressive amendment of the Gravesend and Northfleet club song.....

"Cheer, Cheer, here come the 'Fleet,
 The biggest bunch of w**kers you're likely to meet,
 A ground that's shite, the Red and Whites,
 Are going down again, so...
 Cheer, cheer, 'cos here come the 'Fleet,
 The biggest bunch of w**kers that we'll ever beat."

Finally, on a rather tenuous level, we are going to assume that as another comment on their current tenancy of Watling Street, the United supporters sing *"Show me the way to go home..."* etc - with no more factual a basis other than one of their fanzines has adopted this as its title.

# PORTSMOUTH

Although our contributor bemoans the dilapidated state of Fratton Park and the fact that "they took our Fratton end away", (by removing the roof), in the singing stakes Pompey are amongst the front runners. Being sponsored by a manufacturer of Hi-Fi could have something to do with this, but this is purely speculation on our part. Firstly we must start with Portsmouth's most famous chant, unique in that the "tune" used is the sound of a chiming clock. This is due to the fact that the City is in some way famous for chimes, whether this is as a result of confusion with the "Portsmouth Chines" (beaches) or because of the shipyards' clock we don't know. Apparently this is used rather less frequently these days, as a modicum of on-field sucess is required for the Fratton faithfull to clear their throats.....

> "Play up Pompey, Pompey play up."
> (Repeated ad nauseam)

Going back to the lack of covering over the home terrace, the removal of the old roof over the Fratton End has prompted spontaneous outbursts of "We want a roof" and "We want a Fratton End", both sung to the tune of *"Those were the days my friend"* - Mary Hopkins Euro number.

Obviously proud of their geographical location, the home fans can be heard to sing "Southerners rah, rah, rah, Southerners rah, rah, rah." on the occasion of a visit from northern teams. Again mostly prominent when Portsmouth are winning, this chant has few airings at the moment. On the subject of the City itself, Portsmouth have a slightly amended example of the oft-used "We're by far the greatest team the world has ever seen", replacing "Greatest team " with "Greatest City". This shows a marked lack of enthusiasm towards the playing ability of the eleven players on show. Strangely, this is most vociferously sung on the occasion of away wins, most notably at Plymouth (where they always win, apparently!) as the cavernous roof over the exit promotes a cacophony of sound.

The arrival of ex-army striker Guy Whittingham for the princely sum of £450 prompted a reworking of *"The Quartermasters Stores"*, which had previously been used to value Mick Quinn (his predecessor) at £1,000,000, prior to his departure to Newcastle. This song, used up and down the country to lambast players of a rotund nature (see Brighton), extolled the virtures of the lithe army man with.....

> "He's tall, he's slim,
> He scores more goals than Quinn,
> Whittingham, Whittingham!."

An appropriate song as Whittingham scored (at the Fratton End) within six minutes of his debut apperance as sub against Hull, and went on to score another 14 goals in the next 22 league games, before being eclipsed by the sought after Darren Anderton. (see general section for more *"Quartermasters stores"* efforts.)

Local rivalry with Southampton features prominently, Portsmouth using the derogatory term "Scummer" to denote anything remotely connected to the team up the M27. Visiting players who have had the misfortune to play for Southampton are constantly barracked with the chant of "Scummer, Scummer, Scummer, Scummer". Obviously, on the odd occasion that Southampton are the opposition the plural is used with "vociferous, vitriolic enthusiasm" to quote our respondent. Officialdom also comes in for the same sort of abuse with "You're a scummer in disguise", Portsmouth fans asserting that a "Scummer" is a form of life lower than a snakes belly. The reason for this choice of terminology is sadly not known to us, but an insider notes that Alan Ball was excused this form of verbal abuse despite being Southamptons' midfield mainstay for five years, either side of a brief holiday in Blackpool.

One of the Pompey faithfull's current favourite chants originated just over four years ago when a "legendary" destruction of Southampton by two goals to nil occured at The Dell giving rise to.....

"Scummers 0, Portsmouth 2, Hallelujah"

and......

"Third of the first, eighty eight, Hallelujah"
(Tune: *"Michael rowed the boat ashore"* )

.....the second of the two being the date of the match.

A last chant about Southampton is used when disciplined centre back Neil Ruddock winds up to wallop a clearance in the general direction of Le Tissier, and a mass cry of "HOOF!" goes up from the Chocolate Box end, very subtle!

Away from the Saints and on to (surprisingly) Liverpool who come in for some stick. The following song is used by many teams, but Portsmouth claim to have started the tune back in 1980 after taking 15,000 fans to a cup tie at Anfield on a wet Tuesday night in October. One of our letters poignantly relates how the visiting fans trudged the three quarters of a mile from Lime Street to the ground past, in their eyes, some desperate living conditions. Taking a lofty social stance the throng took up the chant of.....

"In your Liverpool slums, in your Liverpool slums,
You look in the dustbin for something to eat,
You find a dead rat and you think it's a treat,
In your Liverpool slums."
(Tune: *"My Liverpool home"* )

See Man Utd's entry for a plagiarised version of this including a second verse.

We can't leave Portsmouth without referring to the practice of playing Mike Oldfields' supposedly inspiring tune "Portsmouth" over the tannoy when the team run out. A correspondent in WSC finds the impact of this as succesful as "a reggae band at a Ku Klux Klan meeting". There's a tenuous link here between Oldfields' "Tubular Bells" and "Pompey Chimes" - you decide if this is relevent or not!

Bill Beacham

# READING

From the vast sweeping banks of terracing and the majestic soaring grandstands that are Elm Park (erstwhile home of Gabriella Benson) comes a selection of muscial creations that can at best be described as "strange". The normal subjects of rival orientated abuse and encouragement for the team are put aside for a number of sorties into crass stupidity and general silliness. The first example rather aptly illstrates this.....

"In Brisbanes' fair city,
Where the girls are so pretty,
I first set my eyes on sweet Kylie Minogue,
She wheeled her wheelbarrow,
Through streets broad and narrow,
Singing....
I should be so lucky,
Lucky, lucky, lucky".
(Tune: *"Molly Malone"* and, well, the rest's obvious)

A noticeable lack of football related topics in that one, unless you count the oblique reference to the Notts County *"Wheelbarrow Song"*! On a rather more relevant note - though still not a matter addressed by many other teams' followers - the club's kit finds itself the subject of this next piece....

> "Chim-chimminy, chim-chimminy,
> Chim, chim, cheroo,
> We've got a kit that's more yellow than blue"
> (Tune: the ridiculous roof-top number from *Mary Poppins*)

This is a sad reflection on the constant changes in the shirts worn by the Royals players, which have suffered more than most at the hands of the crazed designers since the traditional blue and white hoops met their untimely end. This theme - evidently a contentious subject - crops up again in a particularly repetitive version of *"Yellow Submarine"* - which basically entails singing "We all play in a yellow football strip" several hundred times. The harsh realities of supporting a sadly underachieving team then rudely intrude on the benign and amusing world of your average Reading fan, though as you might expect, things are given a fairly warped slant. The antics of one time goalkeeper Gary Phillips gave rise to this next chant. Although being unequivocally un-Scottish, Phillips' tenancy between the posts was filled with such a stream of horrific blunders and elementary errors that he was soon given the dubious honour of being regaled with....

> "Scotland's number one,
> Scotland's, Scotland's number one".

.....which is about the most searing indictment of a lack of custodial ability which can ever be passed on anyone. On the flipside to Phillips' verbal abuse comes the inevitable hero worship of one of Reading's players - every team has its own prodigal son, and in this case it's Trevor Senior. As well as.....

> "Trevor, Trevor, he's our man,
> If he can't do it,
> No-one can,
> Woooooooooooooooooooooooo!"

.......Senior is given a bit part in this (presumably seasonal) song.....

> "Reading, are you listening?
> It's a goal that we're missing,
> So give it a punt,
> To Trevor up front,
> Scoring in a Winter Wonderland"
> (Tune: *"Walking in a Winter Wonderland"*-
> See Barnets' entry for another version of this)

Quite what form the long drawn out wail takes in the first of these two is a bit of a mystery, as is why Bournemouth merit a mention in this, our last, offering, which is an undeniably unique reworking of a common enough tune....

"I never felt more like feeling quite chuffed,
As Reading win,
And Bournemouth get stuffed,
I'm happy,
I'm really feeling quite chuffed".
(*Tune: "Singing the Blues"*)

So there you have it, a selection of weird and wonderful tunes which give lie to Bristol City's assertion that Reading are "The blandest supporters in the League". The South Bank (for it is they who are responsible for these songs), are another set of supporters whose determination to have a laugh regardless of the circumstances shines through - and they should be suitably congratulated for allowing it to do so.

# SOUTHEND UNITED

The meteoric rise of the Shrimpers up through the Football League has surprisingly not engendered a huge number of new songs - in fact, not one. There are however a few Roots Hall ditties from the fairly recent past which we have received. The first of these is on a subject which is becoming more "popular" in these austere times for our national game, as teams try to upgrade their dilapidated grounds or move to fresh fields. Such actions inevitably anger the traditionalists amongst the supporters of the club concerned, and Southend are no exception. The club's planned move to a multi-million pound super stadium at Basildon was not met with any great enthusiasm, and the following was coined to extoll the virtues of staying put in Southend....

"Oh, we do like to be beside the seaside,
Oh, we do like to be beside the sea,
With our buckets and spades,
And our f**king hand grenades
Beside the seaside,
Beside the sea".
(Tune: *"Oh we do like to be beside the seaside"*)

This is one of the very few occasions where the handwriting of our contributor has defied our efforts to decipher it. "Hand grenades" seemed to be both the only word which rhymed or looked anything like the scrawl we were confronted with and which had even the slightest bit of relevance to the rest of the song - Southend beach being one of the favourite haunts of unexploded wartime mines and other explosives (witness the sunken munitions ship in the Thames Estuary!). If anyone would care to enlighten us as to the actual lyric, we would be most grateful.

The demotion of Colchester United to Conference footballl will have seen this next song made redundant - albeit temporarily - as it was sung at local derbies played at Layer Road to point out the dilapidated state of the away terrace (wooden floored - very quaint!)....

"Layer Road is falling down, falling down, falling down,
Layer Road is falling down, poor old Col U.
Shall we kick it down some more, down some more,
down some more?
Shall we kick it down some more? Poor old Col U".
(Tune: *"London Bridge is falling down"* )

The "Kick it down" part was sung whilst energetically leaping up and down trying to inflict as much damage as possible on the decaying woodwork. Given the equally archaic nature of some parts of Roots Hall, we surmise that this compliment would be returned when it was Colchester's turn to travel up the A12 for the return leg of the big Essex derby.

# SOUTHAMPTON

Given that they play in one of the most accoustically appalling grounds in the League, you could reasonably expect the Saints to have a less than impressive array of songs. However, this is not the case, and thanks to the editorial talent at "The Ugly Inside" we are able to take you on a chronological stroll down the choral avenues which have been explored at the Dell in recent years.

It all started back in the 1960/61 season when local brass band, the Albion, played at the ground for the delectation of the paying public. One inevitable part of their repertoire was *"When the Saints go marching in"*, which was soon latched on to by the crowd. The song really made its mark during the run to the 1963 F A Cup semi final, in spite of the crusade ending in defeat by Manchester United at Villa Park. At about this time, the Dell began to resound to *"Onward Christian Soldiers"*, which had been adjusted to....

"Onwards Saints supporters, marching as to war,
With the cross of Kirby going on before".

The Kirby in question was young George who paused just long enough in Southampton to score twenty eight times in sixty four games before resuming the wandering odyssey which saw him play for nine clubs across two continents in his sixteen year career.

Also popular at this time was *"The Old Brown Cow"*, our knowledge of which does not extend beyond knowing that it was basically obscene and was accompanied by the sound of rattles (!) to simulate the noise of the said cow voiding it's bowels. This prevalent farmyard influence resulted in Wolverhampton's prosaic *"Good bye horse"* song making an appearance or two as well, primarily on the outward journey to away fixtures. Whilst mentioning plagiarised songs, either Middlesbrough F C or the American Civil Rights movement provided the inspiration for the advent of *"We shall overcome"* on the South Coast.

The period 1966 to 1972 was a fruitful one for Ron Davies, the Saints striker who amassed 134 goals for the club during these years. His acheivements were acknowledged by way of...

> "Ronnie Davies is his name, he's the leader of our team,
> The greatest centre forward that the world has ever seen,
> You always can rely on him to score the vital goal,
> And as for Ray Hiron you can stick him up yer la, la,
> la, la, la......" etc
> (Tune: *"Macnamara's Band"* )

Ray Hiron was a contemporary of Davies' - the fact that he played for Portsmouth singled him out for the derogatory mention in this song. His name was, however, interchangeable with that of any centre half who had been made to look somewhat statuesque by the goalscoring adroitness of Mr Davies'.

Springing deftly to the mid seventies, a lyrical reworking of the above tune was used to embody the finest acheivement by a Southampton side, namely the '76 F A Cup win.....

> "'Twas back in 1976, upon the first of May,
> We all went up to Wembley to see Southampton play,
> We showed 'em how to drink the beer,
> We showed 'em how to sup,
> We even showed United how to win the Cup,
> Tra la, la, la, la......" etc

This momentous (for Southampton) event also gave rise to the following.....

> "'Twas back in '76 in the fine month of May,
> The crowd were all roaring and roaring away,
> And when it was over and when it was done,
> We beat Man United by one goal to none.
>
> There stood Lawrie Mac with the cup in his hand,
> Southampton F C, the pride of the land,
> The team to remember, the team to recall,
> Southampton F C, the pride of football".
> (Tune: yet another one to *"The Wild Rover"* )

The "Lawrie Mac" is, of course, Mr McMenemy who stoically led the Saints with some aplomb for a number of years prior to causing havoc on Wearside.

Yet another spurt of inventiveness brought on by Bobby Stoke's goal saw *"The bells are ringing"*, as listed under West Ham, taken up by the Saints following. Naturally, the Hammers "Claret and blue" was altered to "Yellow and blue" to suit Southamptons away colours of the day. Another difference between the two occurs in lines three and four, which in this instance become "Everybody's been knowing, it's up to Wembley we're going, and there's no way of knowing what we're gonna go through." On the subject of the goalscorer that Mayday, Bobby Stokes was immortalised by an adaption of The Equals *"Viva Bobby Joe"* to include his surname.

The Saints next Wembley appearance, for the 1979 League Cup Final, again saw innovative talent at work in darkest Hampshire, the result being.....

"When you walk down Wembley way,
You will hear the Saints fans say,
Who are we gonna stuff?
It's Notts Forest and Brian Clough!"
(Tune: *"The Lambeth Walk"*)

The fact that all these songs originate from the period in which the Saints enjoyed more than their fair share of glory suggests that they are guilty of some blatant bandwagon - jumping (not forgetting that promotion from the Second Division was sandwiched between the two trips to the Twin Towers). Of late, Southampton's dearth of success has negated the creative flair apparent in those heady days. The excellent and caustic fanzine, The Ugly Inside, bemoans this fact and would like to see more inventiveness injected into the Dell's vocal offerings. We can fully sympathise with this attitude as the only recent addition has been the blatantly half inched *"Blue Moon".* And that brings us to the conclusion of our metaphorical amble through the Saints' choral archives.

# Section Two

# London

1) Arsenal

2) Barnet

3) Charlton Athletic

4) Chelsea

5) Crystal Palace

6) Fulham

7) Leyton Orient

8) Millwall

9) Tottenham Hotspur

10) Watford

11) West Ham United

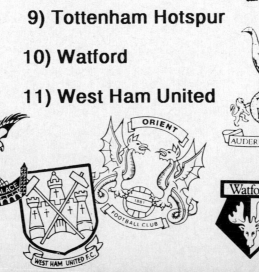

# LONDON

The Capital's relatively high number of clubs have given us perhaps the most "neighbour orientated" selection of songs in any one section. Naturally, with the amount of local derbies played over a season, and the close proximity of the team's, rivalry is intense, perhaps even more so considering that the opposing supporters often live and work in the same area. There is an air of exclusivity about Londons songs, with few references being made - on a regular basis - to teams from other areas, the exception being one or two chants based around a dislike of a couple of the larger clubs from "up North". This local rivallry only exists between clubs of a comparable size and reputation, and is not necessarily based on geographical location. For instance, Chelsea harbour a far more heartfelt hatred of Spurs from North London than they do for Fulham who are virtually on their doorstep. Equally, Spurs (again!) are the butt of the majority of abuse from Upton Park, while Leyton Orient get off without so much as a "We hate Leyton" from the South Bank.

The cosmopolitan nature of Londons population does not appear to be reflected in the roots of the songs, which perhaps reinforces the popular notion that football is predominantly a white, working class game. The majority of the chants are based on themes common throughout the rest of the country, there not seeming to be a particular local favourite. There are a couple of specifically London based tunes, "Maybe it's because I'm a Londoner" and a song from "Me and my girl", but no universally popular song on a parallel with "The Wild Rover" in the North West. London, if anything, appears to export songs to the rest of the country (this being more relevant to the tunes of songs - few seminal chants have started in The Smoke and spread to pastures new) with the traditional Cockney tune of "Knees up Mother Brown" appearing again and again in a variety of areas. With regard to the amount of songs at any one club, Chelsea take the plaudits for having the most of a reasonable length, but Leyton Orient's followers are one of the League's top exponents of the short (apparently pointless) chant.

As a footnote, we would like to clarify the inclusion of Watford in the London section. It is based on the same premise which sees them featured on London Weekend T V (whenever they're doing well) only to be discarded and relegated to the status of "Provincial" when times are bad. Not a particularly relevant point, as we only got the one song from Vicarage Road anyway!

# ARSENAL

The followers of one of the North London giants (sic) with a reputation for not terribly interesting play have sent in a suitably dull selection of songs. In spite of their recent successes, new and innovative chants have not been forthcoming from the North Bank. One of their most popular, and well known, efforts is an updated version of a song released on vinyl in 1971 to celebrate their double-winning season......

"Good old Arsenal, we're proud to say the name,
While we sing this song, we'll win the game,
Good old (insert the name of one of the current purveyors
of tedious football), we're proud to shout the name,
While we sing this song, we'll win the game".
(Tune: *"Rule Britannia"* with words by Jimmy Hill!!!)

Inspired lyrical content or what? Further less than splendid songwriting has given rise to this next chant, which is reputedly aired at Arsenal tube station prior to home matches and on the rare occasions that groups of Arsenal fans encounter like-minded parties en route to away games.....

"Ooh to, ooh to be, ooh to be a, GOONER!"

"Gooner" is the name which supporters of Highbury's XI have coined as their personal appellative, and is presumably a corruption of the Club's official nickname, however, the Concise Oxford Dictionary defines Goon as a "stupid or playful person; subhuman cartoon character" as the origin of this name, this, some would say, having particular relevance to Arsenal's fickle fans.

Next, to a splendidly irrelevant song, performed at away matches when seated in the upper tier of a stand, especially Goodison Park or White Hart Lane.....

"Over and over and over again,
"B'Jesus" said Paddy, "I sing it so well,
I think I'll get up and I'll sing it again",
So Paddy got up and he sang it again,
Over and over and over again".
(Tune: Completely inexplicable!)

This is accompanied with all manner of childlike choreographic goings on, which involve standing up, then sitting down again "en masse". The song is, as one would have expected, repeated for some time until the singers lose their momentum and then perform the less taxing, but equally inane, "Red Army, Red Army, Red Army, Red Army, Red Army, Red Army, Red Army, Red Army....etc".

And that dismal selection was the sum total of the North Bank's creativity - or so we thought until the game at Upton Park in March '92, when the "popular" Hammers chant of "Sack the board" was subtly altered to "Sack the team" as a comment on the dire state of the Claret & Blues - more such invention would not go amiss!!!

# BARNET

Stan Flashman's executive toy has supporters who can reasonably have been expected to have a tidy selection of songs for your delectation - promotion to the Football League seeming to be a fairly egregious occasion which should have spawned a couple of impressive compositions. Things have however remained fairly low-key at Underhill on the creative front, and we have to go back to Barnet's Conference days to find some songs. The first of these is a rather odd two liner thought up after a Hertfordshire Senior Cup final win over Watford...

> "There'll be silver in the boardroom,
> There'll be boardroom in the silver".
> (Tune: more of a chant really, so not much of one)

Most strange - an explanation would be more than welcome if anyone knows exactly what is going on here. Next, a festive offering from Christmas '85...

> "We're dreaming of a nine point Christmas,
> Just like the ones we used to know,
> Where the goalposts glisten,
> And children listen,
> To hear the West Bank in full flow"
> (Tune: *"White Christmas"* )

Why children should stand about listening out for the sound of Christmas revelry coming from Jordan's West Bank is really rather inexplicable - still, it's one of only two songs we've had with a reference to the world of the Druze militia and Christian fundamentalists (see also Meadowbank Thistle) and as such warrants inclusion (all right, we may have misconstrued the "West Bank" reference, but so what!).

And so to the 1986 F A Trophy final between Altrincham and the notoriously boring Runcorn - famed throughout non league circles as having the least vociferous spectators, the least adventurous team and one of the worst playing kits in history (a deeply repulsive yellow and lime green affair). A small number of Barnet fans attended the above match, and by way of derisive sarcasm began to intone "Runcorn, Runcorn, Runcorn" in a markedly boring manner, stretching out the name into a long, monotonous baritone. The uncomprehending Runcorn following, thinking this was a genuine and quite shocking piece of spontaneity, joined in with gusto, much to the hilarity of all who were party to the joke. Another very common song, given a new slant by Barnet following complaints at Whaddon Road, Cheltenham, in 1989 was "Let's go f**king mental" - the contentious word being facetiously replaced with "rather", giving the following audience-friendly version...

> "Let's go rather mental,
> Let's go rather mental,
> La, la, la, la; la, la, la, la."
> (Tune: *"The Conga"*)

# CHARLTON ATHLETIC

In spite of not having had a genuine home terrace from which to extoll the virtues of their team for some six years, Charlton's supporters have still managed to come up with some interesting contributions. Although, at the time of writing, they are not playing at the Valley, their main song revolves around the erstwhile spiritual home, and in particular the Floyd Road, which was the SE7 equivalent of the Anfield Kop in the Addicks' halcyon days.....

"Many miles have I travelled,
Many games have I seen,
Following Charlton,
My only team,
Many hours have I spent,
In the covered end choir,
Singing, Valley, Floyd Road.

Valley, Floyd Road,
The mist rolling in from the Thames,
My only desire is always to be there,
At Valley, Floyd Road."
(Tune: *"Mull of Kintyre"*)

The sixth line has proved somewhat contentious, in that we received another version of the above which reads..."on the travelling road," - this necessitates the use of the word "road" twice in three lines, though, and is therefore the least impressive of the two. With regard to Charlton's huge away following, who take the "travelling road", they are renowned for their lusty renditions of the cry....

"Yippee-yi-yay!
Yippee-yi-yo!"

....which has been culled from some facile fifties song about people riding about on airborne horses, which, if memory serves us correctly, was called *"Ghost Riders in the Sky"*. This is usually performed a couple of times at each away game in order to strike fear and trepidation into the home team - to little noticeable effect in recent years. Another humorous melody to drip from the lips of the boys from nowhere was directed at one half of the current managerial duo during his playing days.....

"Stevie Gritt, Stevie Gritt,
Stevie, Stevie Gritt,
He's got no hair,
And we don't care,
Stevie, Stevie Gritt."
(Tune: *"Hurray, Hurray, it's a Holi-Holiday"* by Boney M.)

Obviously aimed at Steve Gritt's shiny pate, this is performed during the pre-match warm up. Steve seems to take this jovial ribbing in the spirit in which it is intended, usually covering his bald patch with his hands and grinning at the crowd. On one

27

infamous occasion at Home Park, Plymouth, at the end of the 90/91 season, the song was given its best ever airing - in celebration of Steve appearing on the pitch wearing a blonde wig! Before we leave Charlton, we cannot omit the tune played over the tannoy at home games to herald the arrival of the team. Although not generally sung on the terraces (with one or two exceptions), it is notable as one of the few we have received with an instrumental passage. This explains its relative rarity, as instruments are not allowed into the majority of league grounds, thereby denying Charlton's supporters the opportunity to perform the song to the full. It has still managed to become their definitive club song, and has also given rise to a couple of derivatives.......

"When the red, red robin goes bob, bob, bobbing along, along,
There'll be no more sobbing when he starts robbing
his own sweet song,
Wake up, wake up you sleepy head,
Get up, get up, get out of bed,
Cheer up, cheer up, the sun is red.
Live, love, laugh and be happy,
What if I'm blue, now I'm walking through
Fields of flowers.
Rain may glisten, but I still listen
For hours and hours.
I'm just a kid again, doing what I did again,
Singing a song,
When the red, red, robin comes bob, bob bobbing along."

Followed by the sweeping orchestral part, with several of
the above lines repeated in a variety of combinations.

Suffice to say that the aforementioned derivatives generally involve the feathered harbinger of festive cheer meeting his death at the hands of some gun toting psychopath.

Finally, one of the best songs we have had the good fortune to come across - a fine reworking of *"Into the Valley"*, the Skids 1979 hit single, sent in by one of Charlton's most vehement and vitriolic supporters.....Andy Davis!

"Back to the Valley, we're going home,
La, la, la, la, la, la, la, la, la, la, la, (Twice),
We are the Charlton, We are the Reds,
We hate the Palace, we know that they're s**t,
Coppell's a w**ker and Noades is a git,
La, la, la, la, la, la, la, la, la, la, la, (Twice again),
(Brief pause before huge climax...)
Hello! Hello! we are the Charlton!
Hello! Hello! we are the Reds!"

Apparently, this has not caught on too well at Charlton games just yet, but the residents of a certain cul-de-sac in West Kent are getting heartily pissed off with it!

# CHELSEA

Stamford Bridge, a stadium that looks as if it should hold 100,000, actually holds a maximum of 43,900, and rarely sees more than 30,000 - not conducive to a great atmosphere. In spite of this Chelsea have excelled in the creative song stakes, furnishing us with a veritable plethora of material to sift through. From electric fences to banning T.V cameras Ken Bates has always flown in the face of convention and the Sheds' lyrical prowess often reflects this defiance of authority. Typically, and in common with West Ham, a large proportion of Chelsea songs reflect their notorious reputation for violence, which had its heyday in the 1970's as is shown by certain references in the following songs. While most of them can be varied to apply to the majority of clubs, the team that really aggravate the Blues is Tottenham - the cross London rivalry being heightened by Spurs 1967 F A Cup final victory over Chelsea - and for this reason we've used the Spurs version of these variable songs.....

"Hey, Tottenham, do you wanna fight?
Fight the lads in blue and white!
Oh let's fight -
(clap, clap, clap - clap   clap - clap)
Oh let's fight -
(clap, clap, clap - clap - clap - clap)
Well the West Ham ran, and the Arsenal too,
And the Wolverhampton w**kers down at Molineux,
So let's fight...." etc
(Tune: *"Let's Dance"* by Chris Montez)

Other teams apart from Spurs are included in the above, as their fans all had "reputations" at the time of this song's popularity. However, in songs of this nature, the first mentioned team is usually seen as the fiercest rival by those doing the singing. Another reinforcement of the hatred all at Chelsea have for the White Hart Lane brigade is illustrated in the next song. Once again Arsenal and Wolves play bit parts to fill out the song which is specifically aimed at Tottenham, although, perversely, they feature in a last line crescendo.......

"We went up to Wolves,
We took their North Bank,
We came down to Arsenal,
They're not worth a w**k,
So take my advice:
There's nothing so nice,
As kicking the f**k out of Tottenham."
(Tune: *"Messing about on the river"* )

A very apt tune given Chelsea's proximity to the Thames. It's very difficult to fathom out the rivalry which exsists in London as clubs that are geographically the closest are often not chosen as the main target. Obviously league placing comes into play but Chelsea seem to ignore Fulham, who are situated a mere stone's throw from Stamford Bridge. We've also got a shrewd idea that many a Tottenham fan would nominate Chelsea, rather than Arsenal, as the other club they most hate. On with more 'Bridge classics and tales of supposed thuggery outside of the capital get a mention, especially incidents involving that much loved club Manchester United.....

"We are the Shed my friend,
We took the Stretford End,
We'll sing and dance and do it all again,
We live the life we choose,
We fight and never lose,
For we're the Shed, oh yes we are the Shed"
(Tune: *"Those were the days"* - Mary Hopkins)

The United - Chelsea antipathy is again apparent in this next song, which takes the form of two additional verses to United's own song about the European Cup Final. The way in which the song was written out in full by our contributor infers that the original verses are sung by Chelsea, but we think this somewhat unlikely as surely they wouldn't want to sing about another clubs' successes, so we'll stick to the passages relevent to Chelsea's enmity with the Reds....

"They came down to Chelsea in '75,
They took up the North Stand,
The Shed and the side,
But the Chelsea were many,
Too many to ruck,
And the great Man United,
Got battered to f**k!
We went to Old Trafford in '78,
The whole of Manchester was lying in wait,
But Chelsea went mental, 'cos we had our pride,
And the whole of Manchester United died,
Too der loo, too der loo,
And the whole of Manchester United died".
(Tune: as with the original, *"The Wild Rover"* )

Now, for a change, a couple of songs about Liverpool, who it appears were just as unpopular on the Fulham Road as anyone else. The first of these is of interest as it is a unique reworking of a common chant which follows a set pattern elsewhere.....

"In the dark back streets of Liverpool,
Where the Mile End's never been,
Lies the mutilated body of a scouse git,
Where the North Stand kicked him in,
Farewell to Man City, farewell to Liverpool,
We will fight, fight, fight for the Chelsea,
To win the Football League."
(Tune: *"Halls of Montezuma"* )

The Red's Roger Hunt must have been especially unpopular, as he is afforded the recongnition of having his own song...

"Standing on the Spion Kop end,
Throwing bricks at Roger Hunt,
Liverpool is one big brothel,
Roger Hunt's the biggest c**t!"
(Tune: *"Standing on the bridge at midnightt"*)

Lastly, on the "let's have a go at a particular club" theme, it's back to good old Spurs, and a song which also makes an appearance at Upton Park - to add insult to injury, this is to the tune of the cherished Spurs amthem, *"Glory, Glory, Tottenham Hotspur"*.....

"They're turning White Hart Lane into a public lavatory,
They're turning White Hart lane into a public lavatory,
They're turning White Hart Lane into a public lavatory,
And we'll all piss up the wall....sideways!"

Away from Spurs, the "glorify violence" crusade is still in full swing, with a song dating back to 1974 which is sung on the Shed to this day....

"His name is Tommy Baldwin,
He's the leader of our team (what team?),
The finest football team,
That the world has ever seen,
We're the Fulham Road supporters,
And we're louder than the Kop (what Kop?),
And if you want to argue,
We'll kill the f**king lot,
Naaa, na-na, na-na, na,
Na-na, na-na, na-na...." etc
(Tune: *"McNamara's Band"*)

This tune shows a marked turnaround in Chelsea's songwriting attitude, as for once, the virtues of the team and its supporters are extolled in matters other than the ability to kick sh*t out of everyone else. Tommy Baldwin was a long serving Blues striker who amassed seventy four goals in his 187 appearances during eight years at the Bridge.

Moving further away still from the violent tendencies as illustrated in the above few songs, we find the supporters of Chelsea lamenting the occasions that they are required to leave their spiritual home in order to watch the Blues away matches....

"I would grow much weaker,
Weather would be bleaker,
If I spent a week away,
From Chel-el-sea,
Stamford Bridge,
You're the only ground for me,
That's where I go,
It's my home to see Chelsea."
(Tune: *"Peek a boo"* - possibly the thing that Siouxsie and

the Banshees covered not so long ago, although this song was first heard after the original version was released in 1967).

Towards the end of this epic journey through the Stamford Bridge songbook, we come up to date with the infamous celery song - the origin of which is uncertain, but we believe (somewhat controversially) that it could have had something to do with Brighton!

> "Celery, celery,
> If she don't come, I'll tickle her bum,
> With a stick of celery,
> Celery, celery...."

Suitably enough, in the mid eighties when this made its debut, the singers on the Shed brought sticks of celery into the ground to wave about - unbelievably, the Police exhibited their usual tolerance by arresting the carriers of this heinous and potentially dangerous vegetable! The other song which is always thought of as being particular to Chelsea in recent years is "One man went to mow...". First having been performed away at Leeds in 1981, this is now primarily a home orientated song, the Weststanders' being the prime protagonists of the lengthy piece, which culminates with all the singers standing in unison and launching into a concerted shout of "CHELSEA! CHELSEA!". On a rather ecologically unsound basis, there is yet another song which the Bridge faithful claim is one of their most popular chants.

> "Care free, wherever you may be, we are the famous CFC,
> And we'll fight you all, whoever you may be,
> For we are the famous CFC".
> (Tune: *"Lord of the Dance"*)

Quite why chloroflurocarbons are considered to be worthy of idolisation in this manner is beyond us, unless it's because they pose the ultimate threat to mankind which the Chelsea supporters of old would like to have seen themselves as. Finally (at long last), one of the game's most enduring songs, and one of the few "official" club songs which has been enthusiastically taken up by the supporters; it is of course, *"Blue is the Colour"*....

> "Blue is the colour,
> Football is the game,
> We're all together,
> And winning is our aim,
> So cheer us on through the wind and rain,
> For Chelsea, Chelsea is our name!"
> (Tune: *"Blue is the colour"*!)

The actual recording, of course, was considerably longer than this, but the above section is the only part which is regularly heard on the terraces.

# CRYSTAL PALACE

A strange contradiction here as, from the ground which perennially has the worst atmosphere in the first division (and not just when Wimbledon are at home), comes a fairly worthwhile collection of songs. The one which is perhaps best associated with Palace is *"Glad all over"*, which came to prominence during their F A Cup run in 1990. Prior to that, it had been played over the P A at Selhurst as the teams ran out (diagonally!) onto the pitch, accompanied by that delightful eagle figure which we all know and love so well (and if you were really unlucky, the stupid blue bear from the Croydon Advertiser). Having been given hugely unwarranted national press coverage during the Cup run, the song was adopted by all the instant life-long devotees who mysteriously appeared after Liverpool were beaten. These people - who have all had to buy new scarves and those facile little mini-kits to hang in their cars - don't usually manage to stagger past the second chorus of the song before they return to their comatose state..........

"You say that you love me,
All of the time,
You say that you need me,
You'll always be mine,

Chorus:

And I'm feeling...
Glad all over,
Yes, I'm feeling...
Glad all over,
Baby I'm...
Glad all over,
SO GLAD YOU'RE MINE!

I'll make you happy,
You'll never be blue,
You'll have no sorrow,
I'll always be true.

(Repeat chorus)

Other girls may try to take me away,
But you know it's by your side I will stay,
Our love will last now,
'til the end of time,
Because this love, now,
Is only yours and mine.

(Repeat chorus)

Quite what the Dave Clark Five make of having their song hijacked by the occupants of the most overrated football stadium in the country is open to conjecture. They are probably suitably appalled.

The limited merits of this plagiarised ditty are that the supporters occasionally stir from their apathetic slumber long enough to make visiting fans aware of their existence through its performance, and it contains several polysyllabic words, unlike the other chant for which they are renowned - the less than mind expanding....

"Eagles! Eagles! Eagles!"

This is alternatively aired as either "Beagles! Beagles!" when the Palace team contains a number of inexperienced players, or "Cheese rolls! Cheese Rolls!" when the tedium of being a Palace fan becomes too much to bear and a sortie into so called humour is needed to lift the spirits.

This biting wit is also evident in these following chants - the first of which appeared shortly after the final whistle was blown to signal the end of the team's abject humiliation at Anfield in 1989....

"Score in a minute, we're going to score in a minute"
(Tune: *"Juantanamera"* )

Palace's extemely poor Cup record (prior to 1990) gave rise to this.....

"When Jim, goes up, to get the F A Cup,
We'll be dead, we'll be dead"
(Tune: *"Quartermasters Stores"* )

...the Jim in question being the then captain Mr Cannon. The Victoria Ground, Stoke, was also treated to a rare outburst of waggishness in September 1978 (sic?), after Rachid Harkouk and Barry Silkman had been arrested the previous day for allegedly forging banknotes. The Chelsea born midfielder was asked...

"Rachid, Rachid, lend us a quid,
Rachid, lend us a quid".

The timing of this particular song was rather strange, as neither player appeared in this game, and Harkouk had left the club before the start of the season - we fancy our contributor has got his dates somewhat confused!

And finally Palace illustrated their ascerbic sarcasm and acknowledged the lack of circumjacence at Selhurst by somewhat facetiously singing along to the Russ Abbot classic *"Oh What An Atmosphere"*, as it was played over the P A after a 5-0 home thrashing by the future squatters, Wimbledon. So, all in all, a fairly extensive compendium of ditties - which makes the lack of anything remotely resembling atmosphere at Selhurst yet more inexplicable. Of course, now that the bulk of the somewhat transient huge post Cup Final crowds have returned to their former pursuits on a Saturday afternoon, the chances of matters improving have receded considerably, leaving the loyal Eagles to battle on for terrace recognition.

# FULHAM

A club still trying to recover from playing only 87 minutes in the final game of the 82/83 season at Derby, Fulham have a collection of songs that most clubs would be proud of. The majority of these originate from the days before Jimmy Hill and Cabra Estates cast their menacing shadows over Craven Cottage, and hark back to the times of Cup Final appearances and goalkeepers with extremely blonde hair. The simplistic pleasures of this era are amply illustrated by......

> "To Europe, to Europe,
> La-la-la-la-la,
> La la-la-la-la-la,
> To Europe, to Europe,
> La-la-la-la-la,
> La la-la-la-la-la."
> (Tune: theme to *"Top of the Form"*)

This, we presume, became swiftly redundant after Alan Taylor had twice found the net at Wembley, in spite of the efforts of Peter "should have been Swedish" Mellor. Chelsea, actually having lifted the F.A cup, arouse a certain amount of rivaly in their neighbours which surfaces in certain songs. In one we find a reference to Charlie Cooke, The Blues' long serving winger (an eleven year career at the Bridge, interrupted by only a seasons sojourn at Selhurst Park.).......

> "What am I,
> Supposed to do,
> With a girl,
> Like Charlie Cooke.
> (Tune: *"Jesamine"* )

Obviously dated as Cooke ceased playing for Chelsea in 1977. Maybe the next time the SW6 rivals meet the Cottagers will target one of Messrs Jones and co. On a more general level, Fulham have a song aimed at the devotees of their more illustrious neighbours.....

> "As I was walkin' down the Fulham road,
> I met a Blue filth boot boy,
> And he said to me:
> Are you off to see,
> The team they call the Chelsea?
> So I looked around and up and down,
> And I said: you must be joking,
> For if you could see,
> The Fulham F.C,
> You'd know your team needs pokin'"
> (Tune: something akin to the *"United Calypso"*)

The anti-Chelsea bias is also apparent in other songs directed at a variety of players who graced the turf at Stamford Bridge - including an assertion that Alan

Hudson was allegedly a poof as he wore a blue ribbon in his hair. Whether or not this dislike of all things associated with Uncle Ken's club will continue should Fulham become tenants at the Bridge remains to be seen. Confession time now, and the sad inadequacies of our research come to light (see Barnsley), with Fulham's version of *"The Halls of Montezuma"*.....

"From the bright red brick of South West Six,
To the shores of Babylon,
We will fight, fight, fight for the Fulham,
Till we win Division One,
To hell with Liverpool, to hell with Man City,
We will fight, fight, fight for the Fulham,
'til we win Division One."

Why one of the destinations is Babylon instead of the more usual Sicily is beyond our investigative powers - but then, so is why the Mediterranean isle should appear in the other renderings!

As living in the past is currently all that is left for Fulham's supporters, there is one more mention of the epic Wembley trail of '75, and a brief recognition of the part that Birmingham City played in the story (ie losing to Fulham in the semi final).....

"Bye bye Blues,
Bog off Birmingham,
We nearly won the Cup,
We nearly won the Cup."
(Tune: *"Bye bye Blues"!* )

Finally, we cannot leave the banks of the Thames without at least a brief mention of a monstrous version of *"Y Viva Espana"* - this rambles on for three verses, containing numerous references to Alec Stock, Tommy Trinder and other Craven Cottage stalwarts. In the interests of good taste, we have opted to omit these verses, as they really plumb the depths of poor lyrical content and over-sentimental drivel - the following chorus should give you a shrewd idea of the sort of thing from which you have been spared......

"Oh this year we're going to win the Cup,
Hey, viva El Fulham,
Then next year you know we're going up,
Hey, viva El Fulham,
Alan M. is a wonder, that's for sure,
Hey, viva El Fulham,
And Bobby - well do we need say Moore?
It's Fulham por favor."

And you thought a certain large-chinned pundit was the worst thing connected with Fulham. Alan M is, of course, Alan Mullery, and Bobby Moore that well known collector of all manner of bejewelled goodies (World Cups and the like) - both of whom should be mighty proud to have been imortalised in such a song!

# LEYTON ORIENT

After not inconsiderable prompting, the editor of the rather splendid Leyton Orienteer furnished us with a veritable mass of humorous ditties for our (and your) delectation. The majority of these are very succinct and, for the most part, bear little or no relevance to on pitch happenings. Firstly, though, the only couple of songs of reasonable length to emanate from the Brisbane Road terraces. We are reliably informed that - improvised instrumental sequences included - Erasure's "*A little respect*" is a current favourite, as is "*When you're smiling*", though we're not sure whether it is accompanied with any frenzied gesticulation as is the case at Filbert Street (see Leicester).

First, though, to the sixties, and a brief chant to ensure that the Orient faitfhul know exactly where to find their heroes come Saturday afternoon......

"Down the High Road,
Down the Leyton high Road,
Down the High Road,
To see the Leyton Orient."
(Tune: something akin to Chas and Dave's "*Down to Margate*")

Then, on a similar theme to Port Vale's attempts to impersonate five year olds (although perhaps not with the same criminal intent)......

"Orient, Orient, rah, rah, rah!,
Crewe, Crewe, boo, boo, boo!."

Orient have a couple of answer/response type chants, the first of which is presumably a home-only pursuit, with the supporters on the Oliver Road terrace proclaiming the the fact that......

"We're the West Side, We're the West Side,
We're the West Side alcoholics!."

To which the retort from the rest of the ground is.....

"You're the West Side, you're the West Side,
You're the West Side paraplegics".

This, we presume, is a celebration of the admirable ability of the West Side patrons to drink themselves into a stupor prior to attending matches. Even sillier is the inexplicable chant....

"You don't know what a doughnut is, doo dah, doo dah..." etc
(Tune: "*Camptown Races*" )

......which is always the precursor to......

"Silly, silly doughnuts, silly, silly doughnuts".

Continuing the preoccupation with food we have, to the tune of the Dad's Army theme, something akin to Doncaster Rovers mysterious fixation with spongelike comestibles....

"For who do you think you are kidding Mr Kipling,
With your bloody awful cakes?"

The inexplicable nourishment preoccupation continues apace with.......

"Cheese and biscuits, cheese and biscuits,
Vinegar, vinegar!"

And then, still on the "dressing" theme, there's the equally strange.....

"We like beans, we like sauce,
We like sexual intercourse!"

Last on the menu, Paul Gascoigne's favourite snack gets a mention.....

We're all mad, we're insane,
We eat Mars Bars on the train"

This bears more than a passing resemblance to Southend's *"We're all mad we're insane, we watch Southend in the rain".* Less savoury activities perpetrated on B.R's rolling stock are advocated in the following short chant...

"If we lose, if we fail,
Take it out on British Rail!"

Football finally gets in on the act with, in addition to a number of songs of a fairly standard variety directed at the Orient players, a chant in recognition of the teams rather avant garde strip....

"Peter Eustace's red, white and black,
With a stupid yellow number on the back,
ARMY!"

The practitioners of Danny Baker's favourite profession are sometimes put in the spotlight in a less forthright than usual manner with.....

"Who's the self abuser in the black?
Who's the self abuser in the black?
(Repeated ad nauseum)

Still surprisingly on an almost relevant theme, Welsh teams feature prominently in a couple of songs. The first of these is in the form of an addition to the Orient version of the ubiquitous *"Everywhere we go..."* epic (not that it reaches the dizzy heights of the Wolves rendition). The standard lines are climaxed with.....

".....You're invited to Brisbane Road,
To have a row, with Cardiff City,
Ooooooh - we hate Cardiff, and we hate Cardiff,
We hate Cardiff, and we hate Cardiff,
We hate Cardiff, and we hate Cardiff,
We are the Cardiff HATERS!"

The disaproval of all things Welsh then continues on a rather strange tack, with *Land of Hope and Glory* in its "We all follow the Orient..." incarnation including "...over land and sea, and NEWPORT!". Strange in that Newport are, of course, no longer members of the Football League, currently languishing in the Midland Division of the Beazer Homes League. Future meetings between the two teams therefore seem somewhat unlikely, unless Orient follow the footsteps of Preston, Bury and Crewe and take their place in the Welsh cup.

Almost at the end of this trek through the weird and wonderful world of O's lyrical extravagances, we come across something entitled "The mid-table mediocrity song"....

"We're not going up, and we're not going down,
We won't win the League, and we won't win the cup,
We're not good, in fact we're bad,
We are the Orient, WE'RE MAD!"

And finally, one of the very few variations on a much overused theme (which in its original format quite possibly originated in the East End). It is used to accompany place kicks by opposing goalkeepers, and reaches its climax when the ball returns to earth following its journey upfield.....

"Wooooooooaaaaaahhhh...(lengthy pause)...BOINNNNNNNNNG!"

This rather aptly sums up the nature of the singing supporters at Brisbane Road....completely f**king barmy!

# MILLWALL

Like Brighton, Millwall's supporters have been responsiblle for starting one of the game's most enduring chants, which has spread throughout the League over the years since its inception in the late 1970's. It is, of course, the song which is instantly associated with the Den, and is based on Rod Stewart's maritime masterpiece *"Sailing"*.....

"We are Millwall, we are Millwall,
We are Millwall, from The Den,
No one likes us, no one likes us,
No one likes us, we don't care,
We are Millwall, super Millwall,
We are Millwall, from the Den.

One of a number of songs from Millwall which have been committed to vinyl for posterity is *"The Ballad of Harry Cripps"*. Recorded in 1972 (or thereabouts) it is to the tune of *"Danny Boy"* and idolises one of Lewisham's favourite sons, Harry Cripps (bon surprise!) who played for the Lions for thirteen years up to 1974, making 387 appearances.....

> "Oh 'Arry Boy, the fans, the fans are calling,
> From end to end and down the Cold Blow Lane,
> We want a goal, we need your inspiration,
> Oh 'Arry Boy, you know we love you so,
> Throughout the years you've given us your everything,
> Now in return we give this song to you,
> For what you've done is something quite exceptional,
> We pledge ourselves to you our 'Arry Boy."

It's difficult to imagine this resounding around modern day grounds in its entirety, and we assume that it's now been consigned very much to the archives, to be dragged out when a few of the Millwall faithfull are reminiscing in the pub and have had a few beers (and why not?).

The second song to have made it into the recording studio is *"Let 'em come down to The Den"* which, having replaced *"Shoe -shine Boy"* as the pre match fare on the tannoy, has become a firm favourite with the supporters......

> "We're the best team in London,
> No, the best team of all,
> Everybody knows us,
> We're called Millwall,
> Let 'em come, let 'em come,
> Let 'em all come down to The Den."

This is the chorus and, as far as we know, is the only part to have been taken up by the terrace songsters. If you want to know the tune - buy the record!

A phenomenon noted by the editiorial team on a trip to The Den is also perhaps worth noting. It involves basically chanting the name of the team, but the initial consonant is extended to a lengthy "Mmmmmmmmmmmmmmmmmmm......." sound, which is started by various people dotted around the terrace at different times before, rather obviously, concluding with a synchronised "....illwallllllllllll". We didn't notice any signal being given as to when to bring the chant to its climax, so the timing is obviously learnt by any fledgling Millwall fans before they are allowed into the ground.

Other than the above, the ubiquitious *"Mighty Quinn"* has been imported to South London ( *"Come on with us, come on with them, you've not seen nothing like the Milllwall team."* ), as has the rather strange *"Distant Drums"* chant which is listed under the York City entry. As yet, we're not aware of any songs dedicated to that high profile Lion, Danny Baker, having made an appearance, unless that popular Gascoingesque type chant has now made an apperance (Our Danny - overweight? - nah!).

# TOTTENHAM HOTSPUR

In spite of being the footballing equivalent of the BCCI, vis a vis their continuing perilous pecuniary standing, Tottenham, the perennial good-in-the-cup-but-comletely-crap-in-the-league side, have submitted a reasonably worthwhile selection of songs. Most of these, however, do not reflect the ongoing fiscal woes of the one time North London giants. They prefer instead to direct the bulk of their abuse towards Arsenal, predictably enough. The first of these merits inclusion due to its (albeit cursory) mention of our pet subject, drinking.....

> "Show me the way to go home,
> I'm tired and I wanna go to bed,
> I had a little drink about an hour ago,
> And it's gone right to my head,
> Well, wherever I may roam,
> Through land or sea or foam (!),
> You will always here me singing this song...
> We hate Arsenal, and we hate Arsenal,
> We hate Arsenal, and we hate Arsenal,
> We hate Arsenal, and we hate Arsenal,
> We are the Arsenal...HATERS!"
> (Tune: initially *"Show me the way to go home"*, then just
>   a traditional chant)

Whilst it is difficult to improve upon a song, Spurs would think, which infers a deep loathing of the residents of the marble halls, perhaps the drinking could be stressed a bit more..."I had seventeen pints of Ruddles County about an hour ago..." may be more appropriate, or would be more appropriate to be honest! The foam reference is rather difficult to fathom, but could possibly be a failed Scholar enterprise (Irving Expanded Polystyrene Products plc ?).

On a similar theme, the "We hate Arsenal, and we hate Arsenal..." assertion is alternatively preceded by "Away in a manger, no crib for a bed, the little Lord Jesus, he lay down and said....".

The reccuring Anglo-Scottish trait of football songs throughout this sceptred isle is again apparent here, as Spurs consider themselves to be one of the foremost purveyors of.....

> "Oh, it's a grand old team to play for,
> And it's a grand old team to see,
> And if you know your history,
> Well it's enough to make your heart go...ohh...ohh!
> We don't care what the other teams say,
> What the hell do we care,
> For we only know that there's going to be a show,
> And the famous Tottenham Hotspur will be there".

However, our observations would indicate that the White Hart Lane renditions of this lack the intensity of the performances given at Celtic Park, or indeed of those at Windsor Park. Spurs fans then go on to exhibit their own special brand of "humour" with these two shorter chants....

"Hot dog, sausage roll, come on Spurs, score a goal!"

And one of the many "question and answer" type chants which are prevalent throughout the country, where one person will shout "What's the name of the game?" and the remainder of the Shelf will respond with "Soccer, soccer, soccer, soccer". This tends to occur on the not infrequent occasions when Tottenham are playing badly (ie any league game). By way of a moan, this is the only reference to the stupid American colloquial term for the Beautiful Game which we have come across, but this is only to be expected given that Spurs are such strict adherents to the Colonials' money orientated approach to sport.

Lastly, the one song which is associated with Spurs more than any other - perhaps more so in the 60's and 70's than in recent times, it is of course.....

"Glory, Glory, Tottenham Hotspur,
Glory, Glory, Tottenham Hotspur,
Glory, Glory, Tottenham Hotspur,
And the Spurs go marching on, on, on!"

Whether or not the other verses, such as *"My eyes have seen the glory of the coming of the Lord"* are ever actually sung at games is a rather moot point - we imagine that this was the case at some time or other however, as this line has provided the inspiration for one of the Spurs fanzine titles. Yet more trivia, and the song also provided the name for a film, albeit a rather obscure Channel Four effort about three young schoolgirls (!) who were obsessed with the Lilywhites at the time of their double winning triumph (which, of course, perpetuated the long standing myth by happening in a year which started with "19").

Paul Gascoigne is a name synonymous with Tottenham Hotspur everywhere, except here. We have spared you the trite offerings of praise from certain sections of White Hart Lane, which are less in evidence since the infamous "tackle" on Mr Charles.

Further good fortune befalls you, our readers, as you realize that we've gone through the whole Spurs section without mentioning the nauseating *"Ossies' Dream"* - either the official version (because it's crap), or the revised version as adopted by followers of other clubs (because it's anti-semitic crap).

# WATFORD

Given that Vicarage Road has been the starting point for so many auspicious footballing careers (Barnes, Johnston, and that alleged faecial juggler, Steve Harrison), and given the musical talents (sic) of their erstwhile chairman, we may reasonably have expected fans of the Hornets to have come up with an equally innovative variety of songs and chants, but this is not the case. Indeed, there is just one submission from darkest Hertfordshire, and this we had to glean from a copy of one of their fanzines which we happened to get hold of. Even this one song has question marks over the validity of its inclusion as it is so woeful that performance on the terraces is almost inconceivable - but then again, the instigators of "Family Football" have been responsible for so many strange innovations to the game that it is probably sung regularly with deep conviction. Enough pontificating though, and on with.....

> "Ain't we sweet, playing football oh so sweet,
> Oh I ask you very confidentially,
> Ain't we sweet?
> Ain't we nice, from Wilko to Penrice,
> Oh I ask you very confidentially,
> Ain't we nice?
> Just pass the ball in Paul's direction,
> Oh what a goal, ain't that perfection,
> I repeat, that we don't need Dave Pleat,
> Oh I ask you very highly confidentially,
> Ain't we sweet?"
> (Tune: of course, *"Ain't she sweet?"*)

My God...what a paper cupful of crap! Straight out of the fifties and the era of those incredibly poor songs penned by some sadly delusioned fool to a popular tune of the time and afforded the misnomer of "Official Club Song". The players who have had the misfortune to be immortalised in this effort are; Paul Wilkinson (semi prolific marksman and Notts Forest reject) and Gary Penrice, the diminutive Hitler clone who has now taken his goalscoring "talent" on to Villa Park and beyond. David Pleat is, of course, that well known Luton Town manager whose tenure of the Spurs position ended - suitably enough - in circumstances not unrelated to the dubious exchange of money .Mention of Luton brings us to probably the League's most luke warm local rivalry (as opposed to a "heated" local rivalry). The antipathy between Watford and the Hatters would appear, judging by the number of songs we've received from both clubs on the subject, to extend no further than a cursory scrutiny of each others' results in the Sunday papers punctuated by perhaps the merest of grins should either party have suffered a crushing defeat. It certainly cannot be viewed in the same context as, say, Celtic and Rangers or the two Manchester clubs, even Berwick Rangers and Aldershot would appear to harbour more disrespect for each other than do the two giants of football just off the M25 - very poor!

# WEST HAM UNITED

Another club to have suffered greatly under the strictures of Justice Taylor's recommendations which, in this case, have also had an adverse effect on the singing at Upton Park in that their famous *"Bubbles"* anthem has been replaced with *"Sack the board..."* as the most popular song in the East End. The Boleyn Ground, having been unaltered for a number of years, requires a fair amount of work to comply with the farcical UEFA directive, and (surprise, surprise) the supporters of the Hammers are being asked to cough up. Even with average attendances around 20,000 Mr Cearns claims the coffers are empty. Where the £2,000,000 from the sale of Tony Cottee has gone is anyone's guess, let alone proceeds of the hire purchase of Mr Ince....and as for the rent they sting Charlton for? Surely with all this income and respectable gates there shouldn't be any need to fleece the supporters for every penny they've got through the much maligned bond scheme. Anyway, enough of this ranting and raving and on with the matter in hand, and there's only one song with which we can start.....

"I'm forever blowing bubbles,
Pretty bubbles in the air,
They fly so high,
Nearly reach the sky,
Then like my dreams they fade and die,
Fortune's always hiding,
I've looked everywhere,
But I'm forever blowing bubbles,
Pretty bubbles in the air,
UNITED...UNITED...!"
(Tune: *"I'm forever blowing bubbles"* )

Why this song was adopted by the Hammers faithful has proved to be beyond our investigative powers, except to say that it is unique to them. Other clubs when playing the boys in Claret and Blue have been heard, on occasion, to voice the above using *"West Ham"* instead of *"My dreams"* in line five. Probably a fairly apt alteration, except when sung by Fulham or Arsenal supporters. Another song steeped in East End tradition is the following, taken from *"Me and My Girl"*.....

"Bow Bells are ringing, for the Claret and Blue,
Bow Bells are ringing, for the Claret and Blue,
When the Hammers are scoring, and the South Bank
Are roaring, and the money is pouring (!),
For the Claret and Blue, Claret and Blue,
No relegation for the Claret and Blue,
Just celebration for the Claret and Blue,
And one day we'll win, a cup or two, or three,
Or four or more, for West Ham and the Claret and Blue".
(Tune: *"The Bells are Ringing"* )

Surely Gary Wilmot should use this different lyrical arrangement on stage? Next, to one of the many songs we've received which show an admirable attitude to drinking....

> "Man United can stay at Old Trafford,
> And Southampton can stay at the Dell,
> And as for Tottenham Hotspur,
> Well they can go to hell,
> 'Cos we'll all drink to West Ham,
> West Ham's the team for me,
> We'll all drink to West Ham,
> West Ham United F C".
> (Tune: Traditional chant)

And drink they do, to excess, as anyone who has seen the pubs in E13 at 2.30 on a Saturday will testify. Many songs are common to the majority of the Capital's clubs, such as the following, which through extensive research we have found to be perhaps more common at West Ham games than elsewhere, though Chelsea also lay claim to using it on a regular basis.....

> "Maybe it's because I'm a Londoner,
> That I love London town,
> Maybe it's because I'm a Londoner,
> That I think of her wherever I go-oh,
> I get a funny feeling inside of me,
> Just walking up and down,
> Maybe it's because I'm a Londoner,
> That I love London town."
> (Tune: *"Maybe it's because I'm a Londoner"* )

And that's about all the songs which are sung in praise of the Hammers - the majority of the rest being designed to extol the virtues of West Hams' long standing violent reputation, or to abuse other clubs, ie.....

> "He's only a poor little Cockney,
> His colours are Claret and Blue,
> And one day this season,
> For no f**king reason,
> He's gonna kick sh*t out of you!"
> (Tune: *"He's only a poor little sparrow"*)

On a similar theme....

> "Chim chimenee, chim chimenee,
> Chim chim cherroo,
> We are those bastards in Claret and Blue"
> (Tune: Dick van Dyke's rooftop monologue from *Mary Poppins*).

More specifically, one directed at Nottingham Forest.....

"Robin Hood, Robin Hood, riding through the glen,
Robin Hood, Robin Hood, with his merry men,
Steals from the rich, gives to the poor,
Silly c*nt, silly c*nt, silly c*nt".
(Tune: The *"Dennis Moor"* song from Monty Python, which
was in turn pinched from Richard Green's long running Robin
Hood T V series)

This is usually followed up with a chorus of "You can stick your bow and arrows up your arse, stick your bow and arrows up your arse......" etc. Nearer to home now, and a reference to the infamous incident when the United following decided that it would be fun to watch a game at Arsenal from the home terrace...

"The West Ham went in three by three, hooray, hooray!
The West Ham went in three by three, hooray, hooray,
The West Ham went in three by three,
And took the North bank, Highbury,
La, la, la, la, la, la, la, la, la, la, la, la"
(Tune: *"When Johnny comes marching home"*)

There are, of course, many of the more usual shorter chants directed at West Ham's local rivals or opponents of the day. In addition, however, we have found that there is one other universally popular "chant" which probably originated if not at Upton Park, then certainly from East London in general (Orient and Wigan Athletic, with their East End connection, being the other candidates for its inception). It is that extremely irritating accompaniment to goalkeepers' place kicks which, having been prevalent throughout the League for a couple of seasons, is now only performed at clubs who have a high proportion of pre-pubescent ignoramuses among their followers. With the originators now having dropped this, it really is very passe, so give it a rest, eh?

"Whoaaaaaaaaaaaaagh....you're shit, aaaaaaaaaaaaaaagh!"

# Section Three

# East Anglia

1) Cambridge United

2) Ipswich Town

3) Norwich City

4) Northampton Town

5) Peterborough United

# EAST ANGLIA

From the point of view of football songs, the East of the country seems to be stuck in some sort of time warp, with all the clubs (with the exception of relative newcomers Cambridge) having some fairly archaic tunes at the forefront of their choral catalogues. Why this peculiarity should be particulary prevalent in the region is a bit of a mystery, other than the fact that there are apparently no more recent compositions good enough to threaten the popularity of the old chestnuts. Perhaps the average age of the crowds at Carrow Road or the County Ground is markedly higher than the more usual mid twenties mark throughout the remainder of the league - zimmer frames and free bus passes aplenty!

The odd men out are, as mentioned above, Cambridge, who seem to have a much younger following than the majority of other teams. This comes through in their brief but spectacularly strange selection, complete with its references to children's T V programmes and sturdy hooved beasts with impressive antlers.

The relative paucity of singing in the region may suggest a more laid back attitude to supporting activities than elsewhere - any vehement emotion being reserved for local derbies or, in Norwich's case, the visit of any large club. Such occasions prompt the outbreak of all the sad old taunting which has become so unacceptable with the majority of other supporters (Munich songs being a particular favourite of the retards in the Barclay Stand). Relative geographical isolation may go some way to explaining such insularity, but this would be somewhat contrary to our findings in other such cases, where the peculiar location of a club usually leads to several songs in praise of the matter (witness the pride at Plymouth and Aberdeen in their being found at Britain's extremities). Few of our island's popular mainstream chants seem to have penetrated the iron curtain which surrounds the clubs of the region in anything other than a rather cursory manner, Northampton's adoption of the Blaydon Races being the exception here. Perhaps this volume will open the eyes and ears of East Anglia's footballing public to the influences which pervade the rest of the country, if it does, things can only improve.

MOOSE'S
BALL!

FUJITSU

# CAMBRIDGE UNITED

United's relatively short League career has meant that there are very few songs doing the rounds on the Abbey terraces - little or no history to sing about and a lack of a regular decent local derby haven't helped either (even the most ardent of U's fans must find it difficult to get too worked up about the all important grudge matches against the might of Peterborough United, and laterly Ipswich). As with most clubs, though, there is one song at least which lays claim to being vaguely popular, and this is it...

"We beat the Villa,
And we drew at Coventry,
We drew at home to Manchester City,
And when we beat the Swansea,
We won Division Three,
And we've never lost at Wem-her-ley.

Win, win, wherever we may be,
We are the famous C U F C,
And we see you all wherever you may be,
And we'll see you all in the Premier League".
(Tune: *"Lord of the Dance"* )

See what we mean about the lack of history - is drawing at Coventry an acheivement which really merits immortalisation in a song? The tune for the first part of this song is sadly a complete mystery to us, whereas the second verse is just a local variation on a widely used tune. With regard to the last line of part one, this was originally sung as "And we've never lost at Molineux" - this was ditched presumably following a sound gubbing administered by Wolves in the Black Country and replaced for a short time by the inestimable line "And we've never lost in Ouagadougou", which, for the geographically illiterate amongst our readers is the capital of Upper Volta (now known as Burkina Faso). A fourth variation was "And we've never lost on Button Moon", which alludes to the superb children's T V Programme of that name.

Those of you with even a limited knowledge of lower division football will no doubt know about the Cambridge fixation with that large North American mammal, the moose. Why this should be the case is yet another mystery, suffice to say that one manifestation of the craze has seen the universal cry of "You're shit, aaaaaargh!" (aimed at opposing goalkeepers whilst taking place kicks) being replaced by a shout of "Moooooooooooooooooose!".

# IPSWICH TOWN

In spite of having the handicap of being sponsored by the country's foremost suppliers of fertiliser and growth enhancing biodegradable products (ie glorified horse s**t), Ipswich have managed to come up with a couple of interesting songs. One of which, released on record in the days when Bryan Hamilton and Colin Viljoen wore the blue shirts with varying degrees of pride, is yet another which can best be described as strange. It was started by the supporters in Portman Road's West Stand, and goes like this......

> "My name is Edward Ebeneza Jeremiah Brown,
> I'm a football supporter of Ipswich Town,
> Wherever they play you'll find me,
> I havn't missed a game since I was three,
> With my scarf and rattle and big rosette,
> Singing "Where was the goalie when the ball was in the net?"
> Follow the Town, up or down,
> My name is Edward Ebenezer Jeremiah Brown,
> But everyone calls me Ted."
> (Tune: specially comissioned from a Mr G Hicks and best
>  left to your imagination!)

On a far more sensible note, the Division Two championship of 1968 gave rise to this reworking of *"Onward Christian Soldiers"*.....

> "Onward Ipswich Town,
>  Marching to the fore,
>  With the flag of Ipswich,
>  Going on before,
>  Crawford is our leader,
>  Billy is our king,
>  Listen to the North Stand,
>  Listen to them sing."

The players mentioned are Ray Crawford, the prolific goal scorer who returned to Portman Road to spearhead the championship challenge, and Billy Baxter, the not quite so prolific but equally legendary centre half who topped 400 appearances for the Blues. The same season also saw this next song make an appearance...

> "You've got your European,
>  And you've got your F A Cup,
>  But we are Bill McGarry's boys,
>  And we are going up!"
>  (Tune: Rather sadly unknown)

.....Bill McGarry being the manager at the time. This song was slightly altered to have a dig at struggling neighbours Colchester United....

"You've got your Bill McGarry,
And you've got your Ipswich Town,
But Smith and Neil Franklin's boys,
Are surely going down."
(Tune: see the previous version!)

And go down they did - being relegated to the Fourth Division under the stewardship of Manager Neil Franklin. As to the identity of the mysterious Mr Smith, this is possibly Jim Smith (yes, the Bald Eagle) who managed United in the early seventies, although he was in charge at Boston United at the time this song first appeared so it possibly isn't him - well, what do you care anyway?

Finally, something not usually connected with the quiet backwaters of Suffolk - controversy and crowd violence. Town supporters had one song which became their anthem once they were in the First Division - an adaptation of the *"We all agree, Ipswich Town are magic"* theme.......

"I, I R A, Ipswich Republican Army,
Wherever we go, we'll fear no foe,
For we are the I R A".

Innocent enough if you take this purely at face value, but not perhaps the best thing to have chanted at Villa Park in 1975 just after the Birmingham pub bombings. The locals were understandably not too amused at what they saw as support for the Provisionals who had carried out the bombings, and a huge fight ensued with a number of Town fans being arrested purely for singing the song which they regarded as their own.

Over the last few years, singing has been on the wane at Portman Road, and the only notable thing from our point of view is the ongoing campanological contest which has developed between Ipswich and Man City to see who has the more impressive bell ringing supporter. Everton have presumably now entered the fray, with the transfer of Peter Beardsley to Goodison - Esmerelda the Evertonian?

# NORWICH CITY

Norwich fans, without any genuine local rivals to abuse (Ipswich being far too far away to be considered "local"), dedicate themselves to singing several completely ludicrous songs, the first of which lays claim to being the oldest football song still in regular use (unless Sheffield F C were singing the Chip Butty Song in 1857). It was written by one Albert T Smith circa 1890 and was first applied to the Norwich Teachers F C - being adopted by the City team on their foundation in 1902. It did the rounds of the local music halls for some years in the early 1900's, no doubt also cropping up at the many Young Farmers functions held in the area (along with the ploughing matches, largest turnip competitions and the many and varied other rural pursuits).....

"On the ball City, never mind the danger,
Steady on, now's your chance,
Hurrah! We've scored a goal.

In the days to call, which we have left behind,
Our boyhood's glorious game,
And our youthful vigour has declined,
With its mirth and its lonesome end,
You will think of the time, the happy time,
Its memories fond recall,
When in the bloom of our youthful prime
We've kept upon the ball.

(Chorus)

Kick-off,throw it in, have a little scrimmage,
Keep it low, a splendid rush, bravo,win or die,
On the ball, City, never mind the danger,
Steady on, now's your chance,
Hurrah! We've scored a goal.

Let all tonight then drink with me,
To the football game we love,
And wish it may successful be,
As other games of old,
And in one grand united toast,
Join player, game and song,
And fondly pledge your pride and toast,
Success to the city club.

(Repeat chorus to fade...)

Errr...well, it's certainly different if nothing else. The fact remains, however, that apart from *"On the ball, City"*, Norwich themselves don't get a mention which leads us to surmise that Mr Smith didn't fully anticipate his song becoming the anthem of the Carrow Road terraces. Certainly, a few references to Graham Paddon or Kevin Keelan wouldn't go amiss in making the song rather more pertinent to the Canaries, and over the years it could also have been updated to make it vaguely amusing - how about "Channon's missed an open goal" for the last line of the chorus, or the last two lines of the second verse could be "Its been deflected inside the post, lucky Norwich win the '85 League Cup" - endless possibilities, so give up the turnips and improve on this antiquated dirge!

Another oft performed song on the Barclay terrace takes the form of a rhetorical question directed at City's current number one, Bryan Gunn...

"Bryan, what's the score?
Bryan, Bryan, what's the score?
Bryan, what's the score?".

.....in response to which, Gunn will hold up the requisite number of fingers on each hand to illustrate the current state of the game. We would be interested to know with what part of his anatomy Bryan made up the extra "goals" during City's 7-0 F A Cup mauling of Sutton United. Needless to say the Norwich fans only ever ask this question when they are winning - which explains its comparitive rarity. Should an equaliser be scored by the opposition their fans will usually take up the chant to which Gunn responds with a two fingered gesture. Lastly, given the fact that Norwich score a woefully inadequate number of goals, their supporters are often heard imploring....

"Score Norwich, score, once we get one we'll get more"
We'll sing you assembley when we get to Wembley,
So score, Norwich, score"

Many other clubs also sing this, but Norwich's followers are particularly noted for its usage, whatever the nature of the game at which it's performed.

# NORTHAMPTON TOWN

Being as they share their ground with the county cricket team, and that it only has three sides, it would be fair to assume that the Cobblers only have three-quarters of the songs of other clubs. Not true however! - although their submission was not the most extensive we received, it did include one of the most wonderfully stupid songs we came across, in spite of the dubious content of the lyrics.....

"Dan, Dan, the lavoratory man,
He's the leader of the s**thouse gang,
Spends his days cleaning sanitary towels,
And listening to the rhythm of his rumbling bowels,
Slip, slop, a sound is heard, the slip, slop, slip,
Of a slimy turd,
Down, down, into the pan
Oochie, coochie, woochie its the s**thouse gang."
(Tune:unknown,more of a chant really)

Who is Dan? The star of a dubious video retailing at eighty Guilders in Amsterdam perhaps? (see our forthcoming book on coprophilia for further details). The derivation and subsequent usage of this particular song is sadly unknown to us though it would take an extremely good explanation to justify its relevance to the footballing sphere! Perhaps we should be content just to revel in its magnificence before moving hurredly on to the next County ground epic......

"We're from Northampton Town,
So get your knickers down,
La, la, la, la, la, la, la, la, la, la, la,
We're from the Hotel End,
We'll drive you round the bend,
La, la, la, la, la, la, la, la, la, la, la,"
(Tune: *Milord* by Frankie Vaughn)

Although you would surmise that "round the bend" refers to more toilet jollity, the origin of this song is not so straightforward. During a home game versus Brighton in 1968 the men from the Goldstone bought their own mini-skirted cheerleaders (prior to Superbowl extravagance this!!) and being starved of women in Northampton, the resident perverts on the home end were rather keen for a glimpse of the taut young buttocks tantalisingly out of reach. They therefore coined this song in an unsuccessful attempt to encourage the girls to reveal their ample charms. (If one of those lithe limbed nymphets was your mum or sister, we're very sorry for the inevitable embarrassment caused by digging up this unfortunate episode again)

Now, here's a novelty, a substantially different working of *"The Blaydon Races"* popular at the the County Ground in the 70's....evidently the Town followers of this slightly later era had graduated beyond the bottom/toilet fixation of their predecessors.....

"Off we go on Saturdays to see Dave Bowen's aces,
Frankie Large, John Fairbrother, skinheads in their braces,
Eric Ross and Nobby Clarke and Felton pulling faces,
Off we go on Sat-ur-days.....
To see Dave Bowen's aces."

"Felton" is Graham Felton, Town's pacey though generally rather feeble winger of the day, and Dave Bowen the manager who had two spells in charge at the County Ground before ultimately joining the board of directors. Mr Felton evidently did not enjoy the usual praise afforded to popular wingers, as his name crops up again in this next ditty....

"Graham, oh Graham,
We'd climb a million walls,
To get a kick at your balls, oh, Graham."
(Tune: *Mammie*)

It's not clear exactly what he did to incur the wrath of the fans - he was probably just one of those unfortunate scapegoats which all struggling teams have and was unlucky enough to be around during Northampton's relegation years of the late sixties...perhaps he was fat, bald and crap as well!

# PETERBOROUGH UNITED

Not one of the more prolific songwriting clubs in East Anglia - United are going to have to relinquish any ideas they may have had of bettering the inestimable Northampton Town on this score. We've had just a couple of submissions which date from either end of Peterborough's League existence; the first coming from 1956/67 - just prior to elevation to the big time - when they were still in the Midland League. It catalogues the teams F A Cup run, and was to the tune of "The Yellow rose of Texas".....

"It's a non league team called Posh,
That we are going to see,
At London Road we've watched them,
Storm on to victory,
They beat their Midland League mates,
Divisions Two and Three,
A darn good F A Cup run,
We're sure you'll all agree.

It's Billy, Dennis, Andy,
The forwards who combine,
With Cockburn, Shaw and Rigby,
The strongest half back line,
And then there's Barr and Douglas,
Who keep the wings supplied,
With Walls between the uprights,
The foes - they are defied

Corby, Yeovil, Bradford,
Have fallen at their feet,
And now there's Lincoln City,
The latest to defeat,
They're on the road to Wembley,
Via Huddersfield's the way,
With guts and goals and glory,
Posh will show you how to play.

The pre-league nature of these feats defy our usual analysis of the players who are mentioned in the above. We would add, however, that "Posh" is Uniteds' nickname.

The second more recent offering comes from the 89/90 season, when a mid season run of one win in fifteen games threatened to send Peterborough spiralling into a relegation scrap with Colchester United who were marooned at the foot of the table. It was sung between the two sides of the home terrace, and tended to carry on for up to quarter of an hour.....

"The Football League (the Football League),
Is upside down, (is upside down),
The Football League is upside down,
We're going up, with Colchester,
The Football League is upside down."
(Tune: *"When the Saints go marching in"* )

Inspired stuff from London Road and very much in keeping with the optimism in this part of the country. Not that misguided, either, as a recent thrashing of Liverpool bears witness to - a very pleasing event on which to end the Peterborough entry.

# Section Four

# East Midlands

1) Derby County

2) Leicester City

3) Mansfield Town

4) Nottingham Forest

5) Notts County

# THE EAST MIDLANDS

At last - somewhere with a bit of originality, albeit from rather unexpected quarters. With the best will in the world, the County Ground, Filbert Street or Field Mill cannot be considered to be genuine hotbeds of footballing passion, but each has thrown up some half way interesting songs (not much point in recording them here, though, merely flick through the next few pages for explicit and uncensored details).

Perhaps the most notable facet of singing in the area is the rivalry between Notts Forest and Derby County - in so far as Notts County have so far been unable to incur the wrath of their extremely near neighbours and provoke a welter of obscenities from the Trent End. Evidently, it's another example of the so called small fry being ignored by their larger cross-city counterparts, with a more distant club being used as the butt of abuse (evidently, the common ground between the two clubs - ie a certain Mr Clough - has been a contributing factor in the development of the pronounced rivalry between them). Should County ever aspire to even moderate success, then presumably the rapier with of the Forest support with be honed to a fine point at their expense, but until this occurs, any spare City Ground spleen will be vented in the direction of the American forces' erstwhile recreational facility and those that ply their trade thereon.

We were rather sadly only party to one half of the Mansfield - Chesterfield enmity, though on reflection perhaps it is just a one way affair anyway. The Spireites, judging from their fanzine, consider themselves to be part of the South Yorkshire scene when it comes to local rivalry, thereby leaving the Field Mill incumbents in something of a vacuum with no-one to really get up tight about - hence the predeliction for the unspecific beer/deviant sexuality songs at Field Mill.

Leicester City also find themselves out on a bit of a geographical limb, with no-one being near enough to provide a regular target for abuse. Rather sportingly, the supporters of other clubs up and down the country have taken it upon themselves to include City in their songs by way of the ubiquitous "...and Leicester" insertion in the various "We all follow the Wrexham (or whoever), over land and sea, and Leicester!" chants which crop up more or less everywhere. If this is a conscious effort to include a team who would otherwise be conspicuous by their absence in the nations' chants, then it's certainly rather splendid - and given the lack of any more plausible explanation for one of footballs' most enduring conundrums, this'll have to do!

# DERBY COUNTY

Over recent years the fiscal woes of Derby have completely overshadowed the playing side of things and given rise to terrace offerings directed at their former owner, the late Robert Maxwell. The only ones we have received refer to Mr Maxwell's nautical mishap. Most are unpublishable (although fairly amusing - but you have to draw the line somewhere!), however we have included one which aptly illustrates both the hatred of Maxwell by the Baseball Ground faithfull and their guile in turning a timeless classic to suit their own means.......

> "What shall we do with Robert Maxwell,
> What shall we do with Robert Maxwell,
> What shall we do with Robert Maxwell,
> Throw him in the ocean,
> Heave-ho and overboard,
> Heave-ho and overboard,
> Heave-ho and overboard,
> Now the b**tard's drowing."
> (Tune: *"What shall we do with the drunken sailor"* fairly loosely)

Immense wit !! Hopefully now that all the latent talent which was festering in Oxford's first team has been transferred to the Baseball Ground - along with the spare cash from the Manor Ground coffers - they can regroup and try to emulate their early seventies success. Apart from that gem, which must be unique, Derby's Pop side only managed to contribute different lyrical workings to many oft sung tunes. The elucidation of Chelsea's *"One man went to mow"* is notable for the fact that a "Ram" (Their nickname and logo/mascot) is actually doing the mowing, thus saving on petrol - witness the Baaaaseball Ground's pitch........

> "One Ram went to mow,
> Went to mow a Stokie,
> One Ram and his Baseball bat...WHACK!
> Went to mow a Stokie."

Why this song refers to slapping Stoke City supporters (a pastime which we cannot condone) is one of this book's much vaunted "complete mysteries", unless, of course, a "Stokie" is a local derogatory term for a Forest supporter. Derby's well documented dislike of the Tricky Trees manifests itself in the following adaptation of a none too rare song....

> "We hate Nottingham Forest,
> We hate Forest too, (they're s**t!)
> We hate Nottingham Forest,
> And Forest we hate you".
> (Tune: *"Land of hope and Glory"*)

This song is remarkable in that it is the only version we've had where only one club is the target of the abuse - it is usual to list a couple of other clubs, one of which is invariably Leicester City for some reason - though in Derby's case their near neighbours escape the usual abuse meted out by other teams, very surprising!

# LEICESTER CITY

Filbert Street does not reverberate to an awe inspiring selection of songs from the home crowd. There is, however, one contribution which shines out like a beacon amidst the mass of thoughtless mediocrity such as the inevitable chants of "City, City, City..." and "We love you Leicester, we do..."

It is a stunning rendition of the old favourite *"When you're smiling"*, augmented with some rather odd hand waving activities.....

> "When you're smiling,
> When you're smiling,
> The whole world smiles with you,
> And when you're laughing,
> When you're laughing,
> The sun comes shining through,
> But when you're sighing,
> You bring on the rain,
> So stop your sighing - be happy again,
> 'cos when smiling, when smiling,
> The whole world smiles with you,
> Na, na, na, na, na,
> The whole world smiles with you,
> Na, na, na, na, na,
> THE WHOLE WORLD SMILES WITH YOU!"

The last three lines (not counting the rather dubious "Na, na, na bit) are enhanced by, in the first instance, the participants holding their arms aloft with hands motionless, and, during the last line, the arms (and presumably hands) are waggled in synchronisation to add further to the splendour of the occasion. This song started spontaneously some time in 1979 for no apparent reason, and has persisted to the present day, though it is currently struggling to hold its own against the encroaching tide of mindless drivel epitomised by chants of "Blue Army, Blue Army..." and the like. We feel it is the onset of such trash like this, as popularised, not surprisingly, by Arsenal, that will see the downfall of terrace humour well before the advent of all seater stadia as dictated by the Taylor report. The particularly astute members of our readership may have detected, throughout the editorial copy in this book, a less than enthusiastic reception for the coming of the plastic seats and the associated demise of such famous standing choirs as the

Kop, the Stretford End and Wrexhams' Crispin Lane. We feel strongly that songs such as *"When you're smiling"* should be committed to print so that they may be preserved for posterity, and not be forgotten when watching football has become a sterile, soulless pursuit for the extremely wealthy. Lastly, and rather strangely, why hasn't the Filbert Sreet assemblage come up with some songs pertaining to the teams red change strip and Red Leicester cheese? - an odd juxtapostion which deserves some thought, and which would be considerably more justifiable than Maidstone United's dairy product / lunar derived oddities.

# MANSFIELD TOWN

Mansfield's supporters, reputedly once famed for their voluble support, have apparently suffered more than most so far under the draconian new regulations of the Taylor report, and the preceding advent of Colditz style fencing which sprang up at grounds up and down the country (the sole purpose of which seems to be to obscure the view of as many supporters as possible). The terracing at Field Mill was once a veritable hotbed of singing and chanting, with home supporters able to move relatively freely around the ground - either from behind the goal in the North Stand to the extreme southerly end of the West Stand terracing, or vice versa, depending on which end Mansfield were attacking. The fences have now precluded this movement, with the Stags' vocal support now spread more thinly around the ground as a result. The amount of singing has therefore decreased (with however a notable upturn during the current season). One or two songs can still be heard regulary at Mansfield games, one of which is.....

> "Oh when I die (Oh when I die),
> Don't bury me alone (Don't bury me alone),
> Just lay my bones in alcohol (Just lay my bones in alcohol),
> And on my chest lay a barrel of the best (And on my chest
> lay a barrel of the best),
> And tell my friends I've gone to rest (And tell my friends I've gone to rest)."
> (This is repeated over and over until everyone gets
> thoroughly fed up with it - the tune is unknown).

This song is, although unrelated to football, still pertinent to Mansfield, as one of the town's biggest employers is the Mansfield Brewery - like those of Port Vale, Stags' supporters should be congratulated on their preoccupation with drink!

The obligatory "regional variations on a theme" which occur at Field Mill generally have Chesterfield as the butt of the abuse - the Blues being Mansfield's local rivals. Referees who incur the anger of the crowd are addressed with "Who's the Spireite in the black?" - a Spireite being a Chesterfield supporter and therefore a simile for any particulary low form of life.

The football followers' occasional penchant for sexual deviance is evident once again at Mansfield, there being a chant from the mid eighties extolling the virtues of anal sex....

"There's a lady in glitter (There's a lady in glitter),
Who likes putting it up her sh***er (Who likes putting it
up her sh***er),
Singing oh, oh, oh! (Singing oh, oh, oh!)".

And that's it - so in spite of the advent of the fences, Town supporters still find time to get drunk and indulge in unnatural sexual practices - a lesson for us all!

# NOTTINGHAM FOREST

Contrary to popular belief, there are in fact a couple of songs which are intoned by Forest supporters. This is all the more remarkable when you consider their "performance" in the 1991 Cup semi final at Villa Park, when the lack of atmosphere from the Forest supporters on the Holt End was almost laughable. It was hard to believe that supporters whose team was 4-0 up and cruising serenely towards Wembley could have remained in such a completely inert state - the following selection is pretty woeful, but any one of them would have given some much needed atmosphere to a deeply embarassing occasion. One song involves blagging part of a Celtic number (which is slowly spreading throughout the League - Man United and Spurs being a couple of other teams who have adopted it, albeit in a rather more extended version)....

"Through the seasons before us,
Down through history,
We will follow the Forest,
Onto victory."
(Tune: this is a slightly altered four line section from
Celtics' *"Over and Over"* )

Yet more Scottish roots here, as a Rangers song is imported to West Bridgeford, chewed up, buggered about with and spat out as....

"Hello, Hello, we are the Trent End boys,
Hello, Hello, we are the Trent End boys,
We are the best in England,
That no one can deny,
We all follow the Forest"
(Tune: *"Marching through Georgia"* )

Notts County are evidently not considered worthy of abuse, the only reasonably nasty song being directed at Derby, with whom Forest have developed an intense rivallry during the Magpies sojourn in the lower divisions. This is nothing more than standard modification of a very standard theme....

> "There's a circus in the town, in the town,
> Robert Maxwell is the clown, is the clown,
> And Arthur Cox has got the pox,
> And Derby County's going down, going down".
> (Tune: *"There's a Tavern in the Town"* )

And that's yer lot, unless of course, you care to consider one very strange occurrence that we have heard goes on when Forest get a corner in front of the Trent End. Reputedly, the rabid hordes behind the goal eagerly anticipate the forthcoming gentle lob into the visiting keeper's hands by chanting "One, one, one, one, one......" before the kick comes over. Why this should be the case is beyond our comprehension - but then so is why anyone would want to support Forest in the first case - very odd.

# NOTTS COUNTY

With the club being formed in 1862, County supporters have had the best part of 130 years to come up with an amazingly comprehensive set of songs - they haven't done so. What we have had submitted though isn't bad. The first is a brief celebration of the anatomical oddities of County striker Kevin Bartlett....

> "Oh Kevin B (Oh Kevin B),
> Of Notts County (of Notts County),
> Oh Kevin B of Notts County,
> He's got a head like a Malteser,
> Oh Kevin B of Notts County".
> (Tune: *"When the Saints go Marching in"*)

If this is true, Kevin has to be admired at having been able to carve out a reasonably successful career in football in spite of the handicap of having a head with a honeycomb middle that weighs so little (a career which should ultimately end with a return to Kevin's spiritual home town club, York City).

Next, a subtle dig at adjacent Forest based on a little known geographical quirk....

> "Oh Notts County, the only football team to come from Nottingham!".

The relevance of this being that the City Ground is south of the Trent and is therefore actually in the town of West Bridgeford. I suppose this rather obscure reason for slagging Forest is indicative of the relative success of the two clubs - County hardly being in a position to claim superiority over Clough's team on footballing grounds.

The song for which County's supporters have become somewhat notorious in recent years (witness particularly their televised F A Cup game at Spurs in 1991) is another rather strange one......

"I had a wheelbarrow, the wheel fell off,
I had a wheelbarrow, the wheel fell off,
I had a wheelbarrow, the wheel fell off,
I had a wheelbarrow, the wheel fell off...."
(Repeated several hundred times until it gets boring)

The origins of this can be found at an away game against Shrewsbury Town on April 17th 1990; County were embroiled in a promotion dog fight to get out of Division Three, and were desperate for at least a share of the points to keep their challenge alive. They found themselves two goals down and struggling and to make matters worse it was pissing with rain. Somebody - we know not who - started the above chant to sum up the apparently dire state of affairs, with an improvement in the situation following shortly afterwards; Johnson and "Malteser Head" Bartlett pulled back the deficit, County had a valuable point, and went on to clinch promotion, albeit by way of play off wins over Bolton and Tranmere Rovers. The song has, therefore, become inextricably linked with success for County and has been well and truly taken on board as their definitive club song. It has not, though, risen above controversy, with Stockport County claiming (along with an unspecified non league team) to have started the song - Notts County have to be given the full credit though as no-one has written in from Edgeley Park to shed any light on this contentious point. Neither has it escaped the attention of those who would subvert the words into something altogether less wholesome, as the County fans who are partial to a few beers immediately before a game now perform the alternative mix "I've got a full bladder, I want a piss!".

# Section Five

# Humberside

1) Grimsby Town

2) Hull City

3) Lincoln City

4) Scunthorpe United

# HUMBERSIDE

Two teams from this region - Hull City and Grimsby Town - have proved to be the epitomy of the song writing talent which is often forthcoming from the less fashionable clubs (less fashionable than what, we're rather tactfully not going to say!). Both sets of supporters have shown themselves to have both a splendid sense of humour and a real talent for invention. Grimsby's is apparent through their selection of personalised Christmas carols, and Hull through the adaptations of several chart topping tunes. Quite why such talent has manifested itself on the east coast in such a way is (yawn) a complete mystery. The Mariners festive selection seems to have sprung from a conscious effort by the editors of "Sing When We're Fishing" (the club fanzine) to create the songs for their own sake, while the Hull repertoire seems to have been more spontaneous for the most part, although once again the fanzines have played a major part in the creative process. The footballing rivalry between the two sides is not perhaps as intense as we might have expected when you consider the relative isolation in which the clubs find themselves, also, meetings in recent seasons seems to have been in competitions such as the Freight Rover Trophy or Full Members Cup rather than the more pressing affair of League confrontation; should both teams manage to remain in the same divison for a few years (both together that is!), then we're sure that a lengthy repertoire of mutually abusive songs and chants would evolve.

Lincoln City and Scunthorpe find themselves somewhat overshadowed in the company of the above (but then so would a lot of other clubs). City's sterling efforts from their Conference days are worthy of note, whereas Scunthorpe seem to have suffered from the lack of a genuine local rival on which to sharpen their teeth (not helped, we imagine, by the changes in county boundaries which have seen them removed from the footballing hotbed which is South Yorkshire).

As far as common themes being apparent in the regions' clubs, there don't appear to be any. Hull have culled most of the best songs from throughout the country on which to base their efforts, Grimsby's are singularly unique, and the other two are not responsible for anything either distinctive or noticably similar to any other club's songs. In simple terms, Humberside has thrown up some particularly humorous songs, but none of the seminal chants which are likely to spread to other clubs (unless, of course, everyone now jumps on the Christmas Carol bandwagon!).

# GRIMSBY TOWN

Stirring stuff from Cleethorpes as followers of the Mariners have gone completely stupid and taken it upon themselves to be recognised as the supporters with the most impressive array of seasonal songs in the history of the world. While everyone else is content with tuneless renditions of *"Jingle Bells"* as their sole concession to the Yuletide spirit, Blundell Park has become a serious rival to such Christmas iinstitutions as the Queen's Speech and repeats of crap films, with the Harrington/Imperial choirs having come up with a whole catalogue of Christmas Carols. Always tending towards the slightly strange (ie inflatable Harry the Haddocks), things have now got totally out of hand.......

"We're three fans of Grimsby Town,
Follow the team from ground to ground,
Emersons, Applebys, Peter Sheffield,
As long as they don't break down.

Oh, Stevie Sherwood, Ian Knight,
Gilbert does but Cockerill might,
Cunnington, Lever, F A Cup fever,
A vision in Black and White".
(Tune: *"We three Kings"*)

Far too many players mentioned to list them all - suffice to say that these songs were brought out for Christmas 1990, so they must all have been players at that time. Line three of the first verse is, we imagine, a list of some of the coach companies used to transport Mariners fans around the country. Then we have....

"God rest ye, Merry Mariners,
Let nothing ye dismay,
A cup defeat at Blackpool,
Is just another day,
We'll save ourselves up for the League,
And never lose away,
Oh, tidings to Al and the boys, Al and and the boys,
Oh, tidings to Al and the boys."
(Tune: *"God rest ye, Merry Gentlemen"* )

The "Al" in this one is manager Alan Buckley. The next festive favourite to be corrupted by the angelic choristers at Blundell Park is *"Away in a Manger"*....

"Away in the West Midlands, where we love the Police,
A Coventry player is flattened by Rees,
The folk in the away end look down where he lay,
And the referee's red card appears right away,
The home crowd are baying, the ref he awakes,
But the Coventry player, no crying he makes,
We love you, our Tony, and though he's not dead,
We think you are heaven 'cos you stamped on his head."

Hmmmm....must be a rather more recent addition to the Christmas song selection recalling Grimsby's Cup game at Highfield Road in 1991. Still on the yuletide bent we come to......

> "Tis the season to be jolly,
> Fa, la, la, la, la, la, la, la, la,
> 'Tis the season for promotion,
> Fa, la, la, la, la, la, la, la, la,
> Fill the League Cup, sing a carol,
> Fa, la, la, la, la, la, la, la, la,
> Ten pints at the Tilted Barrel,
> La, la, la, la, la, la, la, la, la, HIC!"
> (Tune: *"Deck the halls with boughs of holly"* )

The above glorified one of the promotion seasons but is far more noteworthy for its mention of excessive drinking, a subject dear to our hearts. We assume the Tilted Barrel is a watering hole of note amongst the Grimsby faithfull. There are several more examples of this type of Festive frivolity, some of which go to some lengths to point out the numerous shortcomings of Hull City. Traditionally a holiday fixture, before the FA employed a computer to test the dexterity of fans during BR's immobility, the following is especially apt.........

> "Oh the Hullites get a hiding,
> Every New Year's afternoon,
> And all the teams in Division Two,
> Can say goodbye soon,
>
> For the Tigers are quite hopeless,
> Even their fans are sure,
> That Division Three is where they're off,
> Or maybe even Four."
> (Tune: *"The Holly and the Ivy"* )

That completes the worthwhile seasonal offerings, however the Mariners have excelled in the stupidity department by singing, in full, the following......

> "Meet the gang 'cos the boys are here,
> The boys to entertain you,
> With music and laughter to help you on your way,
> To raising the rafters with a hey, hey, hey!
> With songs and sketches and jokes old and new,
> With us about you won't feel blue,
> So....meet the gang 'cos the boys are here,
> The boys to entertain yooooooooou!"

Yes, it is the theme tune from *"It aint half hot, mum"*, that woeful comedy which brought you Windsor Davies and Don Estelle. One of the most irrelevant songs we've come across from possibly the most irrelevant set of supporters! And that's not all; more concerted lunacy is performed (mirroring similar stupidity which is prone to occur at Tynecastle Park, home of Heart of Midlothian) through - with no

70

apparent rhyme or reason - the advent of one of the game's few terrace dances. This time, it's the T V series Hawaii Five-O which provides the inspiration, with the theme tune being hummed (or sung or whatever) whilst lines of Mariners fans make their way around the terracing miming the paddling actions of the Hawaiian canoeists who appear in the title sequence of the programme. Quite what would happen should Grimsby and Crewe encounter each other hardly bears thinking about, with the "Alexandra Special" going strong at one end of the ground and all manner of Henley-like stupidity at the other!

# HULL CITY

After some careful prompting and a couple of high level executive 'phone calls, the multi talented editorial staff from "Hull, Hell and Happiness" and "Hull to Eternity" (a couple of City's fanzines) came up with a masterly selection of terrace classics. They first referred us to a previous publication which went under the title of "Tiger Mag" (one of the first fanzine type efforts in the country) and a statement therein - made in 1949 - that "supporters at Hull were not known for their vocal encouragement". The vast selection of songs they then go on to detail, however, contradicts this assertion even though, at the time it was made, Boothferry Park's atmosphere was dependent solely on the performance of one song, which was......

"I took my wife to a football match to see Hull City play,
We waited for a trolley bus for nearly half a day,
And when we got to Boothferry Park, the crowds were rolling in,
The bus conductor said to me "Do you think that they will win?",
Shoot City Shoot! Shoot City Shoot!
The grass is green, the ball is brown and we got in for half a crown,
Shoot City Shoot! Shoot City Shoot!
There ain't no guy as sly  as our goalie Bill Bly."
(Tune: *"Sioux City Sue"*)

The mysterious Billy Bly was, in fact, Hull's keeper between the end of the Second World War and 1959 - it being, we fair-mindedly assume, purely coincidental that Hull achieved promotion the year after his retirement. This brings us conveniently to Ken "Waggy Waggy Waggy Oi Oi Oi" Wagstaff's goalscoring reign at Hull which was celebrated with......

"Aye, aye-di-o McKechnie is better than Yashin,
'Waggy is better than Eusebio,
And Carlisle are in for a thrashing"
(Tune: whatever gave rise to the *"We all agree..."* chants)

This song obviously originated after the '66 World Cup, when the foreign players named therein were household names in England. The rather less famous Ian McKechnie signed for the Tigers from Southend in 1966.

The early seventies saw the first outbreak of food related idiocy in the world of football songs (see Doncaster and Orient for examples of more recent strangeness in a similar vein). This first example was imported from Craven Park, home of one of the town's Rugby League clubs.....

"Mrs Hull's sausage rolls are the best,
Mrs Hull's sausage rolls are the greatest,
'Cos they're made from the milk from her tits,
Mrs Hull's sausage rolls fall to bits."
(Tune: *"Here We Go!"*)

The Tigers' fans were prompted to conceive their own song extolling the virtues of other local food outlets - this particular effort still being all the rage on Humberside, and being based on the Welsh hymn *"Bread of Heaven"* (see also Wrexham)......

> "Bread of Skeltons, bread of Skeltons,
> Feed me 'til I want no more, want no moooooore,
> Feed me 'til I want no more"

It goes on to provide a glowing testimony to other comestible-vending establishments in the area in the next two verses, with "Chips from Carvers" and "Pies from Fletchers" getting in on the act. The last (fourth) verse brings the song to a rousing climax......

> "Curries from Shezan, curries from Shezan,
> Make you s**t for ever more, ever moooooore,
> Make you s**t for ever more....
> Na, na, na, na, he's from 'ull and he's from 'ull,
> (Repeat last line to fade)

The last line, which departs from the format followed throughout the rest of the song, would appear to be similar to the "He's a Blade and he's a Blade" goings on as perpetrated by Sheffield United followers - we're not sure, though, which one of the two versions it is more closely related to. We assume that the Shezan is a local curry emporium popular with those that wear the amber and black, and would be interested to know how it compares to the one immortalised in the Wolves *"Everywhere we go...."* song - any information on the relative merits of the two would be more than welcome.

City supporters then elect themselves into an exclusive brotherhood by admitting to having sung a version of the faintly obscene song which we assumed was the exclusive preserve of Hartlepool United.....

> "Eyes right, foreskins tight, arses to the front,
> We are the boys who make the noise, we're only after c**t,
> We're the heroes of the night, We'd father f**k than fight,
> We're the heroes of the Sledmere Fusiliers, (Fusiliers! Fusiliers!),
> We're the heroes of the Sledmere Fusiliers".

Unfortunately, our contributor was unable to shed any more light on the origins of this strange song, which seem destined to remain a complete mystery!

A number of pop songs made it onto the Boothferry terraces, particularly in the 1980's. One or two of these have also sprung up at other grounds around the league (with the obvious changes to make them applicable to whoever is singing them), for example "Karma, karma, karma, karma, karma, come on you 'ull" (To Culture Club's *"Karma Chameleon"* ), and *"Baby Live It Up"* by K C and the Sunshine Band's reworking as "N-na, n-na, n-na, n-na, na-na-na, City's going up, going up, City's going up". The ultimate chart/terrace crossover, however, came in December 1981 when Hull group the Housemartins took *"Caravan of Love"* to number one. Whilst watching their side getting hammered 1-5 at Selhurst Park, thirty or so Hull fans adapted this to.....

"Every woman, every man, Join the transit van from Hull,
Tigers....Tigers,
Every living City fan,  Join the transit van from Hull,
Tigers....Tigers,
I'm your brother, I'm your brother don't you know,
She's my sister, she's my sister don't you know".

A couple of other worthy efforts on a similar tack saw that much abused track *"Yellow Submarine"* change to "We all follow a Black and Amber team, who sometimes play in Green, who sometimes play in Green....." and Bob & Marcia's *"Young, Gifted and Black"* being performed as "Yound, Amber and Black." Also, as mentioned in Burnley's entry, Hull took up the "Um bah bah" chant from *"Double Dutch",* adding the words "The Millwall die, the Millwall die...." when South London's finest visited Humberside in 1983. This proved to be so popular with the Lions fans that they promptly rioted and rearranged a number of the architectural features of the ground in an attempt to get at their rather over confident hosts. There is also yet another variant of Manfred Manns' *"Mighty Quinn",* though not along the usual lines. This time, the song was used to draw attention to a particular physical defect of City striker Frankie Bunn.....

"Come on without, come on within,
You ain't seen nothing like Frankie's chin!"

The chin in question was described by our contributor as "Forsyth-like" - perhaps "Hill-like" would be a more apt football related simile?

Finally, a song which harks back to the more violent days of the 70's, and one which warns against any indiscretions being taken with the boys on Boothferry's Kempton terrace....

"Tiptoe, through the Kempton,
With your boots on,
Get your head kicked in,
So tiptoe, through the Kempton with me".
(Tune *"Tiptoe through the Tulips"*)

This song gives me an excellent chance to really piss off my co-editor by sliding in another mention of Manchester United, who are the only other team we're aware of to use this tune. The Stretford End version, not surprisingly, refers to cross town rivals City, and alters the venue of the tiptoeing to "the Kippax", whilst armed with "a flick-knife, and a sawn off shotgun".

And that just about brings Hull's section to an end, but not before we make mention of the common ground they share with Wigan Athletic through their hatred of Rugby League. Like Wigan, City are often seemingly overshadowed by their neighbouring exponents of legalised thuggery at the Boulevard and New Craven Park - our sympathies go out to them, and we suggest that everyone joins them in a chorus of "My old man said be a rugby fan, I said f**k off, b**locks, you're a c**t.......!!!"

# LINCOLN CITY

Contrary to our experiences of teams newly promoted to the Football League - few of whom have been inspired to come up with any songs by their acheivement - Lincoln's brief flirtation with non league obscurity gave rise to a number of notable contributions. Most of these refer to Barnet who provided the sternest and most sustained challenge to City's objective of regaining their League status. The first of these became popular after the end of the season and following Barnet manager Barry Fry's televised assertion that he would "put his house" on his team going up in place of Lincoln. Short but to the point, the *"Ere we go"* tune was used to acompany the gleeful chant..."Got no house, got no house, got no house." At the point in the season when Barnet's hopes of promotion were finally fended off by the boys from Sincil Bank, (which diligent research has now revealed to have been the final day) Lincoln's vocal support bade farewell to the rotund manager ensconced at Underhill with the pointed........

> "Singing....Bye, bye, Barry, Barry Fry,
> Bye bye, Barry, Barry Fry,
> Bye bye Barry, bye bye Barry,
> Bye bye, Barry, Barry Fry."
> (Tune: *"She'll be coming round the mountain"* )

We have no knowledge of a similar song to welcome Mr Fry to Division Four the following year, however, it is entirely possible that something altogether less savoury was concocted upon his elevation to the higher sphere. City's previous arrival in the Fourth Division by way of an altogether less glamourous route (ie relegation) prompted an acknowledgement of the return to their spiritual home....

> "Division Three, kiss my arse,
> Division Four, we're home at last!"

Back to the early Seventies, when Lincoln were firmly stuck in their rightful division, we come across one of the more usual variations of *"Wandrin' Star"*...this one, though, has a story to it. Having visited Derby in a League Cup 4th Round tie, watching their team achieve a draw and then getting a bloody good hiding from the home supporters, City's supporters formed themselves into a gang to carry out reprisals when the return leg took place. This collection of undesirables soon became known as "The Clan", and in recognition of them, the Railway Terrace where they stood became popularly known as the Clanford End, hence....

> "I was born under the Clanford End,
> I was born under the Clanford End,
> Knives are made for stabbing,
> Guns are made to shoot,
> If you come down the Clanford End,
> We'll all stick in the boot,
> I was born under the Clanford End,
> The Clanford, Clanford End"
> (Tune: *Wandrin' Star*)

# SCUNTHORPE UNITED

With a highest finish of 4th in the Second Division, and never having got past the 3rd round of the (currently) Rumbelows Cup, Iron fans haven't got much to shout about - except, maybe, having the fastest built ground in the Football League, and supplying another point of pilgrimage for all the groundhoppers out there. Despite their lack of success, and having been uprooted from the quaintly named Old Show Ground, Scunthorpe fans have submitted a couple of worthwhile songs. Nicknamed "The Iron", due to the local preponderance of Bessemer Converter related industry, their popular terrace chant revolves around this........

"Any old Iron, any old Iron,
Any any any old Iron,
You look sweet walking down the street,
Hammer in your hand and boots on your feet,
Dressed in style always a smile,
We sing up the Iron,
Oh we don't give a damn,
About Donny Rovers fans,
Old Iron, old Iron."
(Tune: *"Any Old Iron"*)

The inclusion of Doncaster within the song is purely optional, the team mentioned usually being dependent on the opposition of the day, we have used the Rovers as they provide the nearest Football League opposition for Scunny. The other club who are associated with Iron, West Ham, have not claimed a song based around the above so we must assume it is unique to the boys from Glandford Park. This is surprising as it is an old "East End" (of London) ditty. The similarities, however, don't end there as both clubs play in Claret and Blue. Our contributor relates the above as "Early Seventies thug crap" and goes on to state that the "Hammer" in line four has recently been replaced with "Bottle".... really subtle!

During the '77/78 season when much travelled forward Ron Wigg brought his appalling goalscoring record to Scunthorpe (6 in 48 league games) the Doncaster Road End "Lads" regaled him with the following......

"I'm a bow-legged chicken,
I'm a knock-kneed hen,
I aint 'ad a drink since I don't know when,
I walk with a wiggle and a giggle and a squawk,
Doing the Donny Road - Wigg walk."
(Tune: *"I'm a bow-legged chicken, I'm a knock-kneed hen"*)

Ron Wigg became as famous for his alleged drinking abilities as he was for his extraordinary lack of anything remotely resembling footballing aptitude. This admirable skill was honoured in the above song. Although other clubs have submitted variants of the above, this in particular deserves inclusion on its drinking merits. Should Ron Wigg make a comeback the song could still be valid at Glandford Park, as the Rod Mill Terrace (another reference to Iron) can be found alongside the Doncaster Road.

Scunthorpe, in common with almost all other clubs, have a way of telling opposing supporters their name. However their chant is slightly more creative than the usual "United, United" or "City, City" type that is prevalent throughout the other 92 clubs. As we all know, the most unpopular fan worldwide is the chap who stands on the terraces at the Bokelberg Stadium in Moenchengladbach and shouts "Give us a B.....Give us an O....." etc, well, on a similar theme Glandford Park often reverberates to.......

"With an S and a C and a U, N, T,
An H and an O and an R, P, E ,
U, N, I and a T, E, D,
Scunthorpe United - F.C."
(Tune: Traditional Chant )

The final line of this is performed at fever pitch leaving you in no doubt as to who elevon of the players on the pitch represent. The earliest that this could have been used would have been 1958 as prior to this they were known as Scunthorpe and Lindsey United, however the popularisation of this chant has occured over the last ten years or so, as far as we know. That finishes the contributions from this part of Humberside, however we could not leave this mighty club without reference to one of their claims to fame. The joke that asks "Name three captains of England who played for Scunthorpe", is where their name most often occurs in conversation. If you're struggling for the answer then you've forgotten about their illustrious Vice-President, and sometime centre-half, the one and only Mr I.T Botham. The only other time The Iron achieved a degree of notoriety was on the never to be forgotten edition of Grandstand on which the "teleprinter" omitted the first letter of the clubs' name - surely there are grounds for a song in this!

# Section Six

# Yorkshire

1) Barnsley

2) Bradford City

3) Doncaster Rovers

4) Halifax Town

5) Huddersfield Town

6) Leeds United

7) Sheffield United

8) Sheffield Wednesday

9) York City

# YORKSHIRE

The White Rose county has given us an insight into singing throughout the Football League - at the time of writing it can boast both the first and last placed teams with Leeds and Doncaster. We have, as a result, had a wide range of songs, from the strident (and wholly merited) boastings of Elland Road to the completely off the wall ramblings from Belle Vue. In between, there seems to be only one real centre for ardent local rivalry - the City of Sheffield. Apart from the abuse and counter abuse between Wednesday and United, Yorkshire's teams have a fairly ambivalent attitued to each other, which belies the heavy concentration of clubs in such a relatively small area which we would mormally expect to have produced all manner of vitriolic slagging for the various neighbours. There is also a notable lack of common themes throughout the teams - nothing akin to the North West's dependance on "The Wild Rover" or whatever, in spite of our expectations of fifteen or sixteen different versions of "Ilkley Moor ba' t'hat".

A couple of our personal favourites are popular with Yorkshire teams, namely Doncaster's strange preoccupation with the oft quoted spongelike comestibles (a selection of songs this, not just one) and the inestimable "Greasy Chip Butty" song from Bramall Lane. As a result of these two, plus a couple of other noteworthy efforts, we have no hesitation in naming Yorkshire as the most Splendid area in the country for songs. If this assertion is in any doubt, it is only necessary to consider other epics such as Huddersfield's version of "Waltzing Matilda" or the "Park Avenue" song from Valley Parade to see that our wild claim has some reasonable grounds. In answer to the inevitable accusations of editorial bias at this point, we should perhaps point out that it's being written by the half of the editorial duo who is not too kindly disposed towards Leeds United - so there!

On a less contentious tack, it's now time to cast our usual wildy inaccurate aspertions as to why Yorkshire has produced such a wealth of songwriting talent. Well, to be honest, we havn't a clue. It can't be apportioned to the success of the club's breeding a good atmosphere - there has hardly been a glut of trophies at any of the county's stadia in recent years, nor, as detailed above can it be down to a rabid local rivalry, in fact, we have to hold up our hands (in a manner which would do justice to a Filbert Street rendition of "When you're smiling") and say that we've no idea at all, so in place of any such reason, we'll now list eight or nine rather excellent beers which we suggest you try in the near future: Fuller's ESB; Tanglefoot; Theakston's Old Peculiar; Dogbolter; Gale's HSB; Marston's Owd Rodger; Bateman's XXX; any Belgian Trappist beers and finally Pendle Witches Brew. Right, there you have it, completely useless as far as a sociological dissertation as to the derivation of football songs, but totally splendid when it comes to finding a decent pint - what more can you possibly want?

# BARNSLEY

Supporters of the South Yorkshire Reds are apparently still stunned into relative silence by having had to watch their team perform in what must rate as one of football's most unfortunate first team kits ever - the nauseating Shaw Carpets effort of red and white (horizontal) halves, the upper red section being decorated with white stars. As if this was not enough, they have also had to suffer the inane ramblings of Tommy Tyke in their matchday programme - an illiterate buffoon who seems to think that reproducing Yorkshire colloquialisms in print is in some way amusing. In spite of this, they have come up with a couple of noteworthy gems to brighten the gloom, to wit.......

"Oh we ain't got a barrel of money,
But we've got Cooper and Currie,
With Lowndes on the wing,
Doing his thing,
Side by side".
(Tune - surprisingly enough - *"Side by Side"* )

This song celebrates the period up to January 1990 when David Currie took his somersaulting/goalscoring talents to Nottingham Forest. Prior to this he had scored 30 goals in 80 games, alongside the two Steve's, elevating the triumvirate to cult status at Oakwell. The popularity of the above song, though shortlived, was ensured by the local rag's publication of the lyrics. Moving on, and Barnsley's supporters have shown admirable interest in goings on outside their own immediate surroundings by being - as far as we know - the only club in the league other than the two Manchester clubs (and, as we have subsequently discovered, Fulham and loads of others too!) to have adopted the following.....

"From the green, green grass of Oakwell,
To the shores of Sicily,
We will fight, fight, fight for Barnsley,
Till we win the Football League.
To hell with Manchester,
To hell with Liverpool,
We will fight, fight, fight for Barnsley,
Till we win the Football League".
(Tune: *"Halls of Montezuma"* )

This song's usage at Oakwell dates from the late sixties, and has currently slipped from the repertoire - possibly because Barnsley's supporters have conceded that they will have to carry on "fighting" even longer than Manchester United before the championship trophy is secured - and that is going to be an extremely long time indeed.

Other than this the wit of The Reds is tirelessly directed at the players of Rotherham - their local rivals - and, especially during the early to mid-eighties, at one Mr Ronnie Moore......

"Ronnie Moore, Ronnie Moore,
Ronnie, Ronnie Moore,
When he gets the ball,
He does f*** all,
Ronnie, Ronnie Moore".

Ron has however done rather more than "f**k all" with the ball, averaging a goal every two and a half games whilst at Rotherham - a number of which may well have been against Barnsley on the occasion of the big South Yorks derby - achievements which no doubt merited his abuse from the star-spangled Tykes.

# BRADFORD CITY

City's supporters have overcome the handicap of having to watch their team turn out regularly in one of the League's worst kits, with the exception, maybe, of Barnsley - see above, (imagine Chelsea's red and white rhombic effort, but in maroon and amber!) to come up with some stirring stuff. (Bonus points aplenty to anyone who can explain this sudden editorial preoccupation with playing strips!) One submission dates back to the 1960's when Bradford Park Avenue were still going strong, and was dusted off twice a season for the big local derbies....

"Oh, we would go to the Avenue,
But we're not all that hard up,
We would go to the Avenue,
But they've got no beer to sup,
So we'll stay with the City,
Cos we know they're going up,
Yes we'll stay with the City
We'll stay with the City,
We'll stay with the City
Till they're up - right up!".
(The tune to this piece of footballing history
unfortunately escapes us)

A variation on *"Just one of those songs"* also reverberates around the Valley Parade stands....

"We're Bradford City, the pride of the North,
We hate Newcastle, and Leeds of course,
We drink our whiskey, and bottles of brown,
The Bradford boys are in town,
Na, na, na, na, na, na, na, na, na, na, na, na, na."

Obviously Bradford, due to their close proximity to Leeds, consider them their local rivals since the demise of the Avenue in 1970. This explains the reference to West Yorkshire's only first division team (at present) - the mention of Newcastle is, however, a complete mystery, (unless Bradford devotees have a deep loathing of Brown Ale). With a well documented hatred of Leeds prevalent at Valley Parade, we expected a plethora of songs on this subject, the above was sadly the only submission we received, other than the almost obligatory West Yorkshire version of the *"When I was just a little boy, I asked my mother......"* variant on the "Steak and Chips" advert. The words to this can be found under the entry for Leeds, and the Bradford version can easily be ascertained simply by inserting the names of the two teams in the relevant places.

Bang up to date now (well almost), and an adaptation of *"Crazy, crazy nights"* by Kiss......

> "You are my people,
> This is my crowd,
> This is our team and,
> We watch 'em proud
> These are crazy, crazy, crazy, crazy nights...."
> (Repeat numerous times...)

Lastly, a couple of player related chants, the first of which was directed at one time City goalkeeper Phil Liney, who supplemented his meagre professional footballer's wage by crooning tunelessly in local pubs and clubs (including a rather ill advised turn in the supporters' club bar). The followers of other teams were gleefully informed (to the tune of *"She'll be coming round the mountain"*)........

> "We've got the only singing goalie in the land!".

The career of one half of that famous footballing pair of brothers, who eventually gravitated to Bradford towards the end of his playing days, was celebrated with......

> "I met him on a Saturday my heart stood still,
> Da do ron, ron, ron,
> Da do ron, ron,
> Somebody told me that he was evil,
> Da do ron, ron, ron,
> Da do ron,ron,
> Yeah - he's got no hair,
> But - we don't care,
> Cos, when he sticks 'em in,
> We love Ron, Ron, Ron,
> We love Ron, Ron".

It had to happen to someone - and Ron Futcher was the man. No doubt other footballing Rons' have been similarly humiliated, but this is the only one we've been made aware of.

# DONCASTER ROVERS

Rovers' dismal time in 1991 has had the usual effect on the quality of songs which are performed by their supporters; the complete lack of success on the field has forced them to look elsewhere for amusement resulting in an impressive array of ectopical buffoonery. This was admirably illustrated during an early season 2-5 gubbing at Gresty Road by the resurgent Crewe Alexandra. For the most part, standard songs were turned on their heads to reflect the ongoing dismemberment of the team, ie......

> "You thought you had scored,
> You were right, you were right"

along with.......

> "You're going to Wembley, you're going to Wembley,
> We're not!"
> (It was a Rumbelows Cup game).

......and a mournful reworking of the current terrace favourite *"You've lost that loving feelin'"* as "We've lost that Wembley feeling...". An interesting parallel with supporters of Wigan Athletic then surfaced, with the home supporters being asked *"Alex, Alex, do you watch Coronation Street?"*. Encounters between the Rovers and the Springfield Park outfit must consist of a solid ninety minutes of songs about various soap operas! Finally from this game, as the scoreline climbed to the realms of the quintessentially farcical, *"If you're feeling quite embarrased, clap your hands"* also made an appearance.

Away from the doom and gloom of the basement of the Football League, a couple of Rovers players have found themselves the butt of some unique songs. The much travelled Billy Whitehurst (he of the expanding waistline and appalling disciplinary record) is feted with......

> "Wow, fat Billy, bam balam,
> Wow, fat Billy, bam balam"
> (Tune; obviously *"Black Betty"* )

On a more tenuous level, the controversial incident which saw the end of Tommy Tynan's career at Plainmoor is flirted with in the brief......

> "Tommy put the kettle on, Billy take it off again"

Evidently based on *"Polly put the kettle on"*, and a reference to an unsightly electrical appliance mishap in the Torquay dressing room. The details of this particular occurrence are sadly difficult to substantiate - suffice to say that Tynan is not entrusted with the tea making chores at his current club for fear of a repeat performance.

The only more substantial and reasonably sensible song we came across is a throwback to the mid eighties, and is a variant of Frankie Vaughan's *"Milord"* (one of many!).

> "We've travelled far and wide,
> We've been to Merseyside,
> But there's only one place we want to be,

That's on the Belle Vue end,
Where you can stamp your feet,
And all the Barnsley scum lay dead underneath".

Rather unfortunate violent undertones there, and a bit of artistic licence, as the Rovers ground doesn't actually have a Belle Vue end - there's only the Town End and the notorious away supporters enclosure at the Rossington End with security fences which wouldn't have been out of place in "The Great Escape".

A more recently introduced phenomenon is the singing of the unabridged version of William Blake's *"Jerusalem"* by a small group of lunatics at away games. The stirring hymn with its dark satanic mills and other literary verbosity nearly always moves the home congregation to give the choir a rousing ovation on its completion, in spite of the fact that the dramatic denouement is separated from the initial *"And did those feet...."* by some ten or twelve dirge-like verses. This made its debut at Maidstone during a hard fought 1-1 draw - the song being given more immediate relevance by the alteration of one line to *"Maidstone's green and pleasant land"*, presumably similar amendments were made to reflect the venue for subsequent games.

While the team are undergoing a traumatic time, the Rovers supporters are yet another admirable collection of unfortunates who endeavour to lift their spirits by behaving in a splendidly ridiculous manner - this rich vein of idiocy being more apparent than usual on visits to Turf Moor. An Autoglass Trophy encounter saw the following soon-to-be-classics filling the night air... *"Where were you when Elvis died?"*, *"One Nannette Newman, there's only one Nannette Newman"*, *"Bake you a souffle, we're going to bake you a souffle"*, and one that had interesting consequences, *"Would you like a piece of cake?"*. This last effort was performed with accompanying pointing gestures to the Burnley fans to whom the cake was being offered, which was construed in the Police Control Box as "threatening behaviour". The officers on the away end were therefore instructed to stamp out such antagonistic behaviour and were ordered to take the names of some of the perpetrators. It just so happened that the supporters whose particulars were taken shared the same surname, and when another member of the family turned up to sort out what was going on, the Police dissolved into hysterics - a situation which was heightened by a new chant of *"All called Hepworth, you know we're all called Hepworth."*

The unnaturally good humoured way in which the Forces of Darkness viewed these goings on prompted the Rovers fans to attend the following League game at Burnley armed with cakes to offer to the Police on duty - such sponge related tomfoolery inevitably gave rise to yet more songs, the best of which was (to the Lennon tune)....

"And so this is Burnley, and what have we done,
We've lost here already, would you like a cream bun?"

Completely brilliant! Finally, those much maligned black clad upholders of the footballing laws have found themselves the butt of something other than the standard *"The referee's a w\*\*ker"* at Rovers games, with the old chant of *"Oh dear,* *what a referee!"*being revived (we've now found out that this chant is traditional in Rugby League circles - evidently a few Rovers fans spend their Sunday afternoons at Tattersfield!) The linesmen also get a piece of the action, as they are now the subject of *"Mr ..........'s yellow trimmed army".* Obviously, the name of the official fills in the blank, "yellow trim" being a reference to the new style of flag adopted in 1991.

So, all in all, an exceedingly good selection of songs which on its own provides an excellent argument for the survival of the so called lesser clubs in the face of Kelly's fiscal elitism. So much would be lost to the game if the supporters who came up with the above were priced out of the market - can you really see the faceless idiots in the executive boxes contributing anything remotely amusing to the atmosphere of matches in days to come?

# HALIFAX TOWN

Looking likely to be a casualty should the money-minded morons succed with their "Blueprint" of football for the rich (ie the ludicrous ambition of Executive-Box stadia with no fans, except a simpering Elton Welsby), Halifax gamely continue to fulfil their roll of eternal underdogs and, in common with many other "lesser" clubs, breeding grounds for the talent of the future. The continued survival of such clubs is vital, where would David Platt and Peter Beadsley be now if not for Crewe and Carlisle respectively? Hang on, this is getting a bit political and off the point...back to the beneficiaries of Calderdale Council's admirable financial aid scheme; well, they've won nothing of note but nonetheless they are integral to the future wellbeing of football, and have already made an important contribution to popular music, staging a Beatles concert during the sixties, which was filmed and screened as "Live at Shea Stadium". The publicist sadly spelt "Shay" wrong - or are we being just a tad too romantic and confused? Still would have been nice!

The contribution we received courtesy of the splendid "Sound of the Shay" fanzine, consisted of the following excellent reworking of The Scaffold's *"Lily the Pink"* (more Beatles links here!)......

> "We'll drink a drink a drink,
> To Lily the Pink the Pink the Pink,
> The saviour of the Univerheherse,
> 'Cos she invented Tetley bitter,
> And we'll pour it down our throats."

This particular version surfaced in the early eighties, whereas prior to this the last two lines had something to do with unsavoury pranks involving Sulphuric Acid and the rapid reconstruction of various people's features - perhaps this is best left to your imagination! This is, however, another song linking football with drinking, the two most popular and worthwhile pursuits undertaken by the more sensible sections of this country's population.

Now for some contention! The Skircoat choir at the Shay are claiming that the popular "Hee haaw" donkey chant, used to greet opposition players who are

86

large and cumbersome (not to mention totally bereft of footballing skills), originated in Halifax. The Shaymens' supporters started using this around the 83/84 season - when their team was regularly encountering such luminaries as Bill Green of Doncaster and Vernon Allatt of Rochdale - and as far as we are concerned they're more than welcome to take any credit that's going for being the creative force behind the chant. It (the chant) evidently went on to considerably greater heights than Halifax, becoming commonplace in the First Division through the efforts of Tony Adams and the like, before fading into relative obscurity when the aforementioned defender (sic) decided to take a brief holiday in sunny Chelmsford. Meanwhile, back in the Fourth, Halifax fans adopted a new and equally immobile animal with which to compare any suitably inert players - the camel. The one problem with this is that, as yet, no-one there has come anywhere close to perfecting a camel sound, and the Skircoat Choir are rueing the passing of Percy Edwards. If you can do a passable immitation of a camel then rush down to the Yorkshire home of "The World's biggest Building Society" or whatever, where they will be pleased to see you.

# HUDDERSFIELD TOWN

Only a limited response from the Terriers' supporters, but both of their contributions are worthy of inclusion - one being an unusual variation of an old favourite and the other as one of the genuinely unique songs we've come across. First to the Leeds Road re-mix of *"Those were the days"*, the tune to which is often confused with that of Frankie Vaughans' *"Milord"* (not that we're in a position to say which of the two options is correct).

> "Those were the days my friend,
> We thought they'd never end,
> We won the League,
> Three times in a row,
> We won the F A Cup,
> And now we're going up,
> We are the Town,
> Oh yes we are the Town,
> Na, na, na, na, na, na, etc..."

Now, many teams have to go back a few years to find their "glory days" and a subject worthy of singing about, but this effort really takes the biscuit as the achievements listed date from the early 1920's (whilst under the stewardship of the ex Leeds City manager, Herbert Chapman). Still, a recent history which includes a 1-10 defeat by Manchester City is obviously not going to give rise to a great many celebratory songs - perhaps a 2-0 F A Cup win at Hartlepool should have been included in some sort of commemorative chant - but then again, perhaps not.

The occasional antipodean influence on British football songs comes to the fore with this second effort (see also Reading!!) - the West Riding rendition of *"Waltzing Matilda"* being the song in question....

"Waltz in the Cowshed,
Waltz in the Cowshed,
Who'll come and waltz,
In the Cowshed with me?
' cos we'll kick you,
And brick you,
And chop your f\*\*king bollocks off,
Who'll come and waltz,
In the Cowshed with me?"

A little of the original outback naivety may have been lost in the Anglicism of this song - the tale of the Jolly Swagman being turned into an anthem in praise of the latent violence of Huddersfield's home terrace. Whether or not this threatened malevolence has ever actually materialised is open to question - any stories of rampaging Town supporters chopping peoples' genitalia into mincemeat would be more than welcome!

# LEEDS UNITED

After a period of eight years complete inertia in the Second Division, the team from West Yorkshire are beginning to wake up and stake a claim for what they view as their rightful place in the upper echeleons of the football strata amongst the "Big Five" - (when will the media wake up and realize it should be the big six or seven?)

During the recent promotion season, much jollity was seen on the terraces up and down the country. This prolonged and intense period of celebration did not, however, spawn many songs - mainly due to the tremendous popularity of the "official" club song which is sung so often as to stifle other creativity. This song originated during the previous "glory years" when Leeds were the perennial bridesmaids come trophy day. Commissioned as a club song and released by the "Leeds United Football Team and Supporters" on April 15th 1972, the song quickly became indispensable to the Elland Road fans. The 1972 vinyl release was titled *"Leeds, Leeds, Leeds"* although it is more commonly known as *"Marching Ontogether"* - or *"Marching Alltogether"* as some correspondents have claimed, this being the title of one of the club's Fanzines (see Appendix one). Either version fits, but, after a play of the record, we come down firmly in favour of the following.......

"Here we go with Leeds United,
We're gonna give the boys a hand,
Stand up and sing for Leeds United,
They are the greatest in the land,

Chorus

Everyday we're all gonna say,

We love you......Leeds, Leeds, Leeds!
Everywhere we're gonna be there,
We love you......Leeds, Leeds, Leeds!

Marching on together,
We're gonna see you win,
La, la, la, la, la, la,
We are so proud, we shout it out loud,
We love you......Leeds, Leeds, Leeds!

We've been through it all together,
And we've had our up's and down's,
We're gonna stay with you forever,
At least untill the world stops going round,

Rpt Chorus.
(Tune: *"Leeds, Leeds, Leeds".* Original )

Penned by Les Reed and the mysterious Mr Mason, the 1972 Chapter 1 platter is due to be re-released in 1992 to mark its 20th anniversary. This song is one of the more succesful transition's from "official club song" to terrace popularity. Apparently *"Leeds, Leeds, Leeds"* reached number ten in the charts, surely a record for an adopted terrace anthem! The song is very rarely, if ever, sung in its entirety the chorus being the only bit that gets a regular airing. The *"la, la, la"* bit is obviously instrumental on the record, but is used in terrace performances.

On the B side of this inestimable record is something rather creatively called *"Leeds United"*. Being very similar to the A side, it includes such lines as "There's a red headed tiger known as Billy, and he goes like a human dynamo" and "You should see how he runs, speedy Reaney" - although terrace performances are rare (wonder why!) the chorus has, apparently, been heard on occasion.......

"And we play all the way for Leeds United,
Elland Road is the only place for us,
We're heart and soul for the goal that's clearly sighted,
We're out to toast each other from that silver Cup."

The tune, as in the first song, is original and Les Reed had something to do with writing it. These two songs cover the late sixties/early seventies fairly well. Moving swiftly up to date, to the promotion season of 1990, we find an epic song being unveiled for the first time at Elland Road......

"E-aye, e-aye, e-aye-oh,
Up the Football League we go,
When we win promotion,

This is what we'll sing,
We are the champions,
WE ARE THE CHAMPIONS,
Sergeant Wilko's team....Oi !"

Some of our contributors have indicated the last line to be "Sergeant Wilko's King" - we are not sure which is correct and will leave you to decide. After clinching promotion the song became somewhat redundant but has recently been sung vitriolically with the word "promotion" in line three changed to "the Title" as the Elland Road outfit chase English football's major prize. The last line of the song refers to Howard Wilkinson, the manager who is atempting to restore former glories to the club. The "Sergeant Wilko" reference again crops up in the following allegiance shrieking chant....

"Sergeant Wilko's barmy army,
Sergeant Wilko's barmy army,
Sergeant Wilko's barmy army.

There is another song based on these much overused words, but it involves lots of "La's" so we left it out, being bone idle at this point in the creative process.

Leeds were once renowned for their hooligan element, which has been almost wiped out by the club's efforts in recent months, however, they still have a couple of "hooligan" type songs. Although their nearest club is Bradford, followed by the two Sheffield clubs, Leeds' major hate figures are Chelsea and Manchester United. Chelsea, in particular (possibly due in someway to happenings in May 1970), receive season long abuse with.....

"When I was just a little boy,
I asked my mother "What should I be?,
Should I be Chelsea?,
Should I be Leeds?",
Here's what she said to me...
"Wash your mouth out son,
And go get your fathers gun,
And shoot all the Chelsea scum,
Leeds are number one"."
(Tune: *"Que Sera"*)

The last line is often a repeat of the previous one. A song that also booms out from the Kop referring to Chelsea asks.....

"If you're all going to Chelsea, clap your hands,
If you're all going to Chelsea, clap your hands,
If you're all going to Chelsea,
All going to Chelsea, all going to Chelsea, clap your hands."
90  (Tune: *"She'll be coming round the Mountain"*)

This particular ditty is also aimed at other teams, especially Man Utd, who are also on the receiving end of the monotonous and repetitive chant of "Scum, Scum, Scum, Scum". Also on the agenda of anti-team song's, another targeted at Chelsea could be regularly heard during the early eighties........

> "If you're feeling tired and weary,
> And you're wearing Cockney clothes,
> And you want your f***ing head kicked in,
> Just come down Elland Road,
> And as you pass the Gelderd End,
> You'll here a mighty roar,
> F**k off you Chelsea ba****ds,
> We are the Revie boys."

There is another verse after this which is rather too offensive to publish!

As this tome is written, Leeds are currently challenging for the title. Following the injury to Lee Chapman in the F A Cup defeat against Manchester United, a Frenchman by the name of Eric Cantona (Can-toe-nar) was signed to bolster the front line and maintain the drive for honours. Quickly becoming a favourite due to his silky Gallic skills, the Leeds fans have applauded his impact with....

> "Ooh, aah Cantona,
> I said, ooh aah Cantona,
> Ooh, aah Cantona,
> I said, ooh aah Cantona",
> (Tune *"Oops upside your head"*)

This is repeated over and over until everyone is bored or something interesting happens, like a goal, a streaker, or some other noteworthy event.

Lastly we leave Leeds with a couple of one liners performed this season. The first was in the match away at Upton Park, where the away terrace affords a view that could be best described as crap. The Leeds contingent, still recovering from the previous nights' excesses (for it was New Years Day), voiced their dissaproval at this injustice by taking up (to the tune of British Airways "Fly the flag" advert)....

> "Can we see the goal,
> Can we f**k, can we f**k."

Secondly, when playing Aston Villa at Elland Road the whippet like winger Tony Daley (no relation to Arthur) was subject to some subtle satire with....

> "Stupid haircut, stupid haircut, hello,
> Hello, stupid haircut, stupid haircut."

This is obviously a reference to the rather strange way that Mr Daley wears his hair - which, for the benefit of the uninitiated, is somewhat akin to that of Soul-to-Soul's lead singer, Jazzie B.

At this point we leave Leed's due to lack of time and space. However one of our contributors from Leed's notes that he could fill a whole book with songs from the Yorkshiremen. We wish him luck!

# SHEFFIELD UNITED

The supporters of Sheffield United (evidently a collection of disaffected cowherds and wild bootleggin' mid western pioneers) have rather splendidly altered the words to John Denvers *"Annie's Song"* to suit their own deviant ends. It's performed with boundless enthusiasm, particularly at away matches, and goes like this......

"You light up my senses,
Like a gallon of Magnet,
Like a packet of Woodbines,
Like a good pinch of snuff,
Like a night out in Sheffield,
Like a greasy chip butty,
Oh Sheffield United,
Come thrill me again...
La la la la la la la OOAARGHHH!"

Magnet is a particularly nasty local ale, inflicted on the unwary by Tadcaster's John Smiths brewery.

This song is universally known within footballing circles as the *"Chip Butty Song"*. Joking apart, this, although rather brief, is extremely good. Few supporters who have heard Harry Basset's travelling army in full voice giving the above an airing can fail to have been impressed, however grudgingly. The last line bears some similarity to the end of Man United's *"Pride of all Europe"*, and it was somewhat amusing during the Old Trafford encounter between the two sides to hear the opposing sets of supporters trying to outdo each other in producing the most vicious angst-ridden roar (Sheff United winning hands down).

Apart from this, United supporters have a couple of songs dedicated to the team's erstwhile prolific strike partnership of Brian Deane and Tony Agana, the first being as follows...........

"Deano, De-e-eano, we want a goal and we want one now!
Not one, not two, not three not four,
We want a goal and we want one now."
(Tune: *"Banana Boat Song"* )

Furthermore, there is the following singularly impressive "song" which is one of the more idiosyncratic contributions we have received.

> "Brian Deane and Tony Agana,
> Wibbley, wobbley, woo,
> Put them together and what do you get?
> Wibbley, wobbley woo!"

This is an updated derivation of the late seventies/early eighties version which applied to the Blades' dynamic managerial duo of Harry Haslam and Danny (Stockport County) Bergara, and will now require updating since Agana's departure:......

> "Harry Haslam, Danny Bergara,
> Iggledy, Boggledy, Boo,
> Put them together and what have you got?
> Iggledy, Boggledy, Boo!"

Note the subtle variation from *"Iggledy, Boggledy, Boo"* to *"Wibbley, Wobbley, Woo"* - evidently the Bramall Lane faithful have taken note of the excellent series of stories which have appeared on packets of Jelly Babies in recent times and include all manner of wibbley, wobbley jelly references!

Further classics from the Shoreham Choir include part of an old Batchelors number (written by "Silverstein") which was sung for light relief during a tedious goalless draw with West Brom at the end of the 87/88 season.

> "There are green alligators and long legged geese,
> Some humpty back camels and some chimpanzees,
> Some cats and rats and elephants,
> But as sure as you're born,
> You'll never see no unicorn".

And that's not the end of the stupidity - during a Group Cup (fine competition!) match away at Grimsby, the travelling United supporters amused themselves by leaping about, pointing at each other and, in an increasingly ridiculous atmosphere, singing "He's a Blade and he's a Blade and he's a Blade and he's a Blade and he's a Blade" (etc ad nauseam) to the tune of the *"Can Can"*. Along similar lines, Adam and the Ants *"Prince Charming"* was adapted and is performed with similar pointing style activities to enhance its farcical propensities...

> "He's a Blade, OOOH!, he's a Blade, OOOH!,
> Shefield Wednesday are nothing to be scared of."

Back to 1977 for the next, and a song culled from the followers of the then dominant French team St. Etienne. These supporters were apparently renowned for chanting *"Allez les verts"* (Come on you Greens) whilst waving small, plastic French tricolors. United devotees took this up by taking advantage of the prevalence of small, plastic Union Jacks at this time (Jubilee year, remember!) and began to wave these around whilst intoning *"Allez les Rouges"*. According to our contributor, who was present when such auspicious happenings took place, this was a deeply impressive sight - we somehow doubt it!

It is with some relief that we are able to turn to United's last bizarre offering, concerning that legendary journeyman Barry Butlin, who, during his two year sojourn at Bramall Lane, was serenaded with the following....

"Eye, oh, Barry, Barry Butlin,
Barry, Barry Butlin, we love you".

The last line was strictly subject to the quality of Mr Butlin's performances, and thus, on the downside, was altered to *"Barry, Barry Butlin, you are shite"*, on all occasions other than the twelve when he managed to find the net (deeply impressive background research or what; this figure not taking Cup games into account).

So there you have it, an extensive record of some of footballs more silly songs, as perpetrated by some of football's more silly supporters. Still, all credit to them for taking both themselves and the game in general in a superbly light-hearted manner - more of this would be very welcome.

# SHEFFIELD WEDNESDAY

Sheffield's other club - they of the potentially huge crowds and large contingent of Charlton rejects - have sadly not come anywhere near to matching their local rivals in the terrace song department. We did however have a contributing letter which reveals some songs almost unique to the mid-week team. The first of these, popular in and around the early eighties, is....

"Bob Bolder in the net (Bob Bolder in the net),
Mark Smith in defence (Mark Smith in defence),
Andy Mac scores a goal (Andy Mac scores a goal),
Everbody rock and roll! (Everbody rock and roll!)".
(Tune: Unknown)

We can only assume that the "Andy Mac" mentioned above was (and probably still is) Andy McCulloch, who played 122 league games for Wednesday scoring 43 goals between 1979 and 1982. The other two players identities are no mystery - Bolder going on to notoriety with Charlton, and Smith onto worldwide acclaim as frontman for popular indie band The Fall (in actual fact, he was a local lad who worked on Saturdays and thus was forced to ply his trade at Hillsborough). Next, a tune with some particularly suspect rhymes....

"We've travelled far and wide,
We've been to Merseyside,
But there is only one place I wanna be,
And that is Hillsborough,
Where it is magnifique,
And all the Blades lay down on their faces".(!!!!)

This is to the tune of Frankie Vaughan's *"Milord"* and is let down rather badly by the strange last line. To sample a more coherent version of this song, turn to the entry for Doncaster Rovers. Further cross referencing, and to the Sheffield version of Hartlepools' strange "pervert" song, which was sung by Wednesday fans briefly during the early eighties.....

Me mother's a whore on Liverpool docks,
Me uncle's a flasher,
Me aunty's a slag,
The Yorkshire Ripper's me dad,
Na, na, na, na, na, na, na, na, na, na, na, na, na."
(Tune: *"Just one of those songs"* )

Wednesday claim to have been the first supporters to use *"Singing the Blues"* in a football context (a la Man City and everyone else with a hint of blue on their shirts).

This was first heard in the late seventies, and took off at Hillsborough to such an extent that it was actually recorded by Terry Curran in 1980. The part of the son aired was.....

> "I never felt more like singing the blues,
> The Wednesday win, United lose,
> Oh Wednesday, you've got me singing the blues."

There is another variation on this theme which harks back to the dark days when violence was rife at football....

> "I never felt more like kicking a red,
> In the head, until he's dead,
> Oh Wednesday, you've got me kicking a red".

However, after some degree of tergiversation (flash or what!), the former interpretation has been adopted as the more popular of the two.

Another football song peculiar to the city of Sheffield (as far as we're aware) is an adaptation of Jeff Beck's *"Hi ho, silver lining"* which has been corrupted to "Hi ho, Sheffield Wednesday" or "Hi ho, Sheff. United" depending on where the singers' loyalties lay. This is apparently performed at any social occasion in the city (ie wedding receptions) where a) the song is played and b) where the two opposing sets of supporters are represented. The two versions are sung as a contest to see which camp can out-sing the other. Highly entertaining!

# YORK CITY

Those who are destined, through no fault of their own, to follow the Minstermen have presented us with a lengthy, if rather unoriginal, precis of the lyrical abilities of the Bootham Crescent faithful. For the most part the songs are the usual regional derivatives of much more widely used chants - for instance *"Halls of Montezuma"* appears in all its glory with the first line "From the banks of the River Ouse....". Also *"In Dublins Fair City"* and *"We're on the march..."* receive similar treatment.

One submission does however differ significantly from its more usual format, this being Manfred Manns *"Mighty Quinn".* Whereas up and down the rest of the country this is used solely to assert the popularity of any player who happens to go by the name of Quinn (with the exception of Millwall), City have given it a uniquely different slant.....

> "Come on without, come on within,
> You've not seen nothing like a City win".

Not only does this display the total lack of basic English grammar which we thought was our own preserve, but it infers that a "City win" was once a thing of great rarity and not inconsiderable beauty which was to be cherished - which presumably dates the song to any of the six seasons that resulted in an application for re-election to the Football League.

Another almost unique effort stems from Jim Reeves' mid sixties recording of *"Distant Drums"* (again, see Millwall!), and sees scatalogical schoolboy humour being imported onto the terraces from behind the bike sheds. There would appear to be no justification behind the adoption of the chant - it's not even vaguely amusing, but in years to come it may be seen by scholars as a significant contribution to the development of the terrace subculture (all right, there's absolutely no chance whatsoever of this happening, but we've got to try and make York's entry a reasonable length somehow!)......

> "I hear the sound of distant bums,
> And do they smell?
> Like f**king hell!"

Yes....very interesting indeed. Moving hurredly upwards from the depths of lavatorial humour we find, well, nothing, and so this is obviously an excellent point at which to end.

# Section Seven

# The North East

1) Darlington

2) Hartlepool United

3) Middlesbrough

4) Newcastle United

5) Sunderland

# THE NORTH EAST

Right, there's enough misinformed pontificating about the insular abuse which is the extent of songwriting in this region in the following few pages, so, in this brief forward perhaps we can take a more detached view of life on the terraces of the North East.

One thing which was very evident in the contributions we received was that the generally accepted view of Tyne/Tees/Wear side as the epitomy of footballing passion is not wholly true. Fair enough, there is a fair proportion of mutually exclusive slagging which goes on, but nothing which seems to transcend the all consuming hatred of the club's immediate neighbours. Whereas in the rest of the country, the terrace composers target a wide range of unfortunates at which to direct their bile, things remain rather incestuous in the land of the Blue Star. This lack of variety leads us to question the right of the North East to lay claim to it's usual "footballing hotbed" epithet. Perhaps it is the relative (current) dearth of success for the clubs which precluded the arrival in our P O Box of hundreds of impassioned songs and chants from Roker, St James's and Ayresome. It would seem that there is no shortage of latent fervour waiting to come to the fore given the slightest encouragement (ie the "Big Match" mentality), but generally, things seem to be a bit low key.

The songs we were made aware of fall in to the standard "something old, something new, something borrowed...." selection which is common up and down the country (not much sign of "something blue" though, it has to be said!). Traditionalists can always point to "Blaydon Races" as being the definitive summation of the area's songs, but it is now so widespread, and so infrequently performed with any feeling on Tyneside, as to almost have become one of the game's "general" songs instead of solely a stirring Geordie anthem. Innovation is the preserve of the Roker hordes, "Only fools rush in", and an update of (yes, you've guessed...) "Blaydon Races" being examples of newish efforts to have risen to prominence. The second example is, though, yet another of the area's preoccupation with itself, and is an apt illustration of the rather blinkered attitudes which are prevalent. This is not to say that we're not in favour of songs directed at local rivals. but a degree of national awareness would have made the songs of the North East all the more noteworthy.

With only Middlesbrough showing any signs of a prompt return to former (long term) glories, there seems little chance of matters improving and horizons being broadened in the near future. It seems sad that the once committed crowds have drifted into such apparent apathy, and we can only hope that the region's teams see an upturn in fortunes, with the associated improvement in vocal encouragement which such successes would lead to - the national game would be the richer should this happen.

# DARLINGTON

Somewhat untypically, we'll start this section with a north eastern team who's supporters haven't got some forty six verse opus for us to transcribe. In fact, there's very little from Darlington at all apart from all the usual general songs adapted to fit their own achievements / local rivals. One thing that is worthy of note however is that Darlo fans used to delight in singing one of Tenpole Tudors finest offerings *"Wunderbar"*. Not a great deal of point in listing all the words though - as *"Wunderbar"* is the only one! Apart from this, there came to light an original 60's club song, which may be worthy of consideration for future renditions on the terraces of the Feethams Ground. For your delectation we reproduce the lyrics below which, though woefully bad, should inspire Darlo fans to take up their traditional battle hymn.

> "Come on the Quaker men, the boys in black and white,
> We cheer them every morning, every afternoon and night.
> Feethams is our home ground where we score goals galore,
> And now we shout for more, more, more!"
> We'll sing Darlington forever,
> We'll sing Darlington forever,
> We'll sing Darlington forever,
> As the Quakers go marching on, on, on!"

This was especially commissioned as the club song (again!) and we believe that it is to the tune of *"John Brown's Body"* (or *"Glory, glory hallelujah"*, whatever you want to call it). This gem of information was received from, of all things, a Portsmouth supporter who professes a close affection for the Quakers and who heard the above being performed at Farnborough during a GMVC game.

The only other reasonably interesting contribution from Cleveland is an aria dedicated to mid 70's goalkeeper Alan "the Cat" Ogley. Somewhat predictably, it goes......

> "Ogley, Ogley Ogley,
> Oi, Oi, Oi,
> Ogley, Oi,
> Ogley, Oi,
> Ogley, Ogley, Ogley,
> Oi, Oi, Oi!"

Is this where this strange cry first saw the light of day? If you've ever been to an English League game, you must, at some time or another, have heard this being chanted - little realising that it celebrated the career of one of the game's most illustrious of stalwart custodians!

Our contact inside the Feethams Ground, evidently aware of the awful social stigma attached to following Darlo, made the specific request that we keep his name a closely guarded secret and that we credit "The Tin Shed" for his contribution. This seems fairly reasonable, so, the above songs were all sent in by "The Tin Shed"! (is that OK, Steve?).

# HARTLEPOOL UNITED

Surprisingly enough, Hartlepool haven't allowed themselves to get caught up in the usual North East frenzy of manically obsessive abuse aimed at their local rivals (ie Darlington), at least, none of the songs we've received have shown this to be the case. Instead, they have set out their stall as the most obscene supporters in the country with songs containing as many references to deviant sexuality as possible (some of which are based on recent headline making news stories - see below). The first offering not wholly for family consumption is...

> "Me brother's in borstal,
> Me sister's got pox,
> Me mother's a whore down Hartlepool docks,
> Me uncle's a pervert
> Me aunty's gone mad
> And Jack the Ripper's me dad,
> La, la, la, la, la, la, la, la, la, la, la, la, la".
> (Tune: *"Just one of those songs..."*)

With a couple of subtle amendments, this was also performed by those that saw fit to follow Sheffield Wednesday in the early eighties. The next offering from the Victoria Ground is a further piece of nastiness with absolutely no relevance to football. If anyone knows who or what the "Millhouse Fuseliers" were, perhaps they'd let us know (was it the soldiers who hung the famous monkey?).

> "Eyes right, foreskins tight,
> Bollocks to the front,
> We are the boys who make no noise,
> We're only after c**t,
> We're the heroes of the night
> And we'd rather f**k than fight,
> We're the heroes of the Millhouse Fuseliers
> Fuseliers! Fuseliers!
> We're the heroes of the Millhouse Fuseliers".

More frivolous fun in the next one, which (and this is a complete stab in the dark) may bear some relevance to the Cleveland Social Workers row of recent times. On the other hand, it may not, and it's just a further gratuitous bit of extreme naughtiness - still, all good fun isn't it?

> "We've got a nasty reputation for soliciting little boys,
> For raping old age pensioners and nicking kiddies toys,
> We're the perverts of the nation, we're the worst you've ever seen,
> We're a pack of foul mouthed b**tards and they call us Hartlepool!".
> (Tune: *"Macnamaras Band"*)

So there you have it - Hartlepool get our vote as unequivocally the fans with the most irrelevant and unecessarily smutty songs in the League - well done lads!

# MIDDLESBROUGH

Unlike their counterparts at St James' Park, the adherents to Boro's cause on the Holgate End are fairly prolific in the song writing department. We're not sure why this inequality should be the case - as current success doesn't appear to be a prerequisite for having a voluble following, so the Maggies relative silence cannot be attributed to their present dire predicament (Kevin Keegan - ha!). Firstly, 'Boro have adapted the Scottish national team's anthem *"Flower of Scotland"* (see elsewhere for the "proper" words)....

"Oh team of England,
When will we see
Your like again.
We've fought and died for,
And we'll do the same again.

Let's turn against them,
Who? - the Geordie armies,
And send them homewards,
To think again.

The terrace is bare, now,
They've ran away once again,
We will defend thee,
And be that team again."

Questionable literacy there (*"They've ran away"*?) but a noble effort nonetheless. On a more standard tack, the next number is directed at a local rival (at least, Boro regard them as local rivals, even though the butt of their criticisms are dismissive of such an attitude)....

"Sunderland, don't bother me,
Sunderland, don't bother me,
Go away, come back another day,
Don't bother me."
(Tune: *"Hey girl, don't bother me"* )

More neighbourly antipathy next, but with a different target......

"When you're feeling lonely, and when you're feeling sad,
Just go down to the Holgate, and you won't feel so bad,
'Cos when you're in the Holgate, you'll hear a mighty roar.....
F**K OFF YOU GEORDIE B**TARDS,
AND DON'T COME BACK NO MORE!"
(Tune: *"Macnamaras Band"*)

Another song which is almost uniquely attributable to the exponents of the vocal arts at Ayresome Park is a verbatum performance of *"We shall overcome"* - the song which became synonymous with the Civil Rights movement. The words are very boring though, so we're not going to put 'em in! Next, the Tyneside fixation rears its ugly head again with an amalgamation of two popular songs....

"All the Geordies went to Rome, just to see the Pope,
All the Geordies went to Rome, just to see the Pope,
All the Geordies went to Rome, just to see the Pope,
And this is what he said....

Who's that team they call the 'Boro,
Who's that team they all adore,
And they play in red 'n' white,
And they're f**king dynamite,
And we'll support the 'Boro evermore."
(Tune: *"Ally's Army"*)

Lastly, a tale of strange goings on in the Clive Road stand. Ayresome Park is, apparently, none too conducive to good acoustics for singing, so the wooden floor of the stand is put to "good" use to help in creating a supposedly intimidating atmosphere. This basically entails the use of two stamps of the feet on the said floor followed by a single clap to recreate the drum rhythm which precedes the Queen track *"We will rock you"*. After several minutes of this behaviour, the previously seated supporters stand up en masse and launch into a raucous chant of *"We will, we will rock you"* (occasionaly changed to *"F**k you"* if the circumstances decree). This is specificaly designed to put the opposition into a state of trauma - thereby facilitating an easier game for the 'Boro. The only real parallel we can find to this sort of thing are the seal imitations in the Trinity Road stand at Villa Park, turn excitedly to Aston Villa's entry for details........

# NEWCASTLE UNITED

One of the game's most famous clubs has fittingly given us one of its most well known and enduring songs - we refer of course to *"The Blaydon Races"*. It has been adopted and adapted by other club's supporters up and down the country - always the sign of a classic - but will always be associated primarily with the Geordies even though it has rarely been performed in fitting circumstances by its originators in recent years as the side have struggled to live up to their past reputation. It would appear, however, that the reliance on this one song has been to the detriment of the evolution of any others - as we have not been made aware of anything else which is similarly capable of evoking high passion on the Gallowgate End. We could, perhaps, have reasonably expected far more songs to have come in from Newcastle, either in praise of the many famous players who have worn the black and white over the years or, more recently, to express dissatisfaction with the current dire plight of the club. Other than the nowadays mandatory *"Sack the board"* chant, however, it seems that *"Blaydon Races"* remains the sole vehicle for the expression of emotions by those who follow United. Apparently, the last time that it was sung with anything like an appropriate degree of passion was at Wembley in 1976 during the League Cup final as "the Toon" went down 1-2 to Manchester City. The song reputedly rambles on and on for hours, but we have only been able to ascertain the definitive words to the first verse and the chorus - which everyone knows anyway.....

"We went to Blaydon Races,
'twas on the ninth of June,
Eighteen hundred and sixty two,
On a summer's afternoon,
We took the bus from Bamburghs,
And she was heavy laden,
Away we went along Collingwood Street,
That's on the road to Blaydon.

Oh, me lads,
You should have seen us gannin',
Passing the folks along the road,
Just as they were standin',
All the lads and lasses there,
All with smiling faces,
Gannin' along the Scotswood Road,
To see the Blaydon Races."

The countrywide derivitives of this basic theme are many and varied. For the most part, the first verse as detailed above is never sung by anyone other than Newcastle supporters, and it is the second section, which amounts to the chorus, which has been reworked on numerous occasions. Such adaptations invariably include the substitution of lines three and four by "The fastest team in the land, you should've seen us running", and the insertion in line seven of the name of a road which is in close proximity to the home ground of the plagiarists. The last line is also always changed to "To see................'s aces", with the name of a manager or famous club personality being used to fill in the blank. The Geordie colloquialism "gannin'" rarely makes it in to the rewritten songs - which is just as well as it probably wouldn't cross over into any other dialect with any great success.

We were greatly surprised that the supposed intensity of feeling on Tyneside didn't manifest itself in a wide range of disparaging songs about the other clubs which form the North East's much vaunted "footballing hotbed" - obviously there is no love lost between the different sets of supporters in the area, but we must assume that any such enmity is voiced at St James' through nothing more interesting than the bog standard chants which can be found almost anywhere - for instance, we imagine that such gems as "F**k off, 'Boro!" are fairly prevalent whenever the Teessiders pay a visit.

And that's it as far as Newcastle go. If you're a Geordie disappointed at the unbalanced view, in this inestimable publication, of the amount of songs sung by the clubs in your region (ie bugger all by the Toon and loads by Sunderland and Boro') then don't blame us. All your fanzines were sent our standard begging letter asking for information - but it would appear that none of the people responsible for them could be arsed to do anything and as we only include authenticated contributions our hands are tied - hence your brief entry.

# SUNDERLAND

Vaux breweries, loads of unemployed shipbuilders and quite a few people who have a serious attitude problem about Newcastle supporters - sums up Sunderland fairly succinctly. Whilst few of the songs which are traditional on the Fulwell End mention either Vaux or P45's, the majority usually carefully manage to sneak in one or two references to the much hated Geordies from St James' Park. Read the following song lyrics and see if you can spot anything that seems vaguely anti-Newcastle - bet you cant!

To the tune of *"The long and the short and the tall"*...

"F**k 'em all, f**k 'em all,
John Tudor, MacDonald and McFaul,
We'll never be mastered by those black and white b**tards,
'Cos Sunderland's the best of 'em all."

See, nothing too outrageous in that one...try this for size, though, a fairly recent masterpiece to the tune of the *"Blaydon Races"*......

"We went to Wembley Stadium on the twenty eighth of May,
Heading for the play-offs, Swindon Town to play,
We didn't win a trophy and we didn't win a cup,
But what really riles the Geordies is we lost and still went up.

It started twelve days earlier, at St James's Park,
We were soaking, we were freezing, but wasn't it a laugh,
The Geordies made some noise that night, they really made a din,
But you should have heard the Leazes End when Marco's goal went in.

They came on from the Milburn Stand, the Gallowgate the same,
Dancing round like arseholes as they tried to stop the game,
They got stopped on the halfway line by all the boys in Blue,
We just had one complaint that night, they should've let them through.

"The Mackems finished under us, the play-offs are all wrong,
"We were six points ahead of them" the Geordies moaned along,
The tears they flowed into their broon, oh how the Geordies cried,
But I'll never forget that magic night Newcastle f**king died."

This splendid song basically tells the story of Sunderlands' play-off victory over Newcastle at St James' Park which sent them to Wembley and headlong into the Swindon controversy. Newcastle's supporters, naturally fairly pissed off at seeing their team go behind to a Gabbiadini strike (ref "Marco's goal"), invaded the pitch and tried to get the game abandoned. They streamed on from all corners of the ground and made towards the jubilant Mackems in the Leazes (away) end but were intercepted by the police in the middle of the pitch and turned back; result stands, wild celebration in Sunderland and a sudden upturn in the suicide rate on Tyneside.

As all Sunderland and Newcastle supporters will attest, there is only one "derby" game in the North East - Middlesbrough are condescendingly referred to as "Yorkshire reject b**tards", and not just by these two teams. In spite of this xenophobic attitude on Tyne/Wear side, 'Boro fans have a full repertoire of abusive songs directed at both their "neighbours" - as you will have noted from their entry. If you hadn't gathered this already, Sunderland fans are generally known as "Mackems" when born and bred in Sunderland itself, although the Rokerites do have the odd Geordie supporter, this term usually being reserved for Newcastle followers. This explains why the Roker faithfull never sing "We hate Geordies", whereas Middlesbrough fans do! To finish this sociological analysis of North Eastern politics, one song which sums up the deep divisions rather aptly:

"With an N and an E and a "Wubble-U, C,
an A and an S and a T, L, E,
a U, N, I and a T, E, D,
Nowoaotlc United...F**K OFF!!!!".

A fairly recent addition to the songs performed on the Fulwell (and presumably on away terraces up and down the country which Sunderland visit) is indicative of the current trend for taking up songs without any direct footballing connotations (ie *Blue Moon; Bright Side of Life; A Little Respect* etc)....

"Wise men say, only fools rush in,
But I can't help falling in love with you,
Wise men say, only fools rush in,
But I can't help falling in love with you,
SUNDERLAND! SUNDERLAND!"

This is another song which has given rise to a fanzine title - *"Wise Men Say"* being one currently available (see APPENDIX 1 for other examples of this phenomenon).

Lastly, there is a startling piece of originality currently popular at Roker Park, in that the otherwise pathetic chant of "Red Army, Red Army, Red Army" (or Blue/Green/Yellow/Maroon army etc) has been completely rewritten to give the much more impressive "Red and White Army, Red and White Army........" etc. Hopefully, this is a sign of better things to come!

# Section Eight

# The North West

1) Blackburn Rovers

2) Burnley

3) Everton

4) Liverpool

5) Manchester City

6) Manchester United

7) Oldham Athletic

8) Wigan Athletic

# THE NORTH WEST

The dense concentration of clubs in this area has lead to a number of songs being based around a couple of popular tunes. The region's songwriting capacity would have been halved (almost) if "The Wild Rover" had never been written, as it seems almost obligatory that clubs found in Lancashire (well, in Lancashire before the county boundaries were redefined!) must have at least two songs based around this traditional folk ditty.

Manchester's footballing rivals have often found common ground in the songs they sing - more often than not, with one or other of the pair claiming to have been the instigators of a song, and their opposite numbers to have stolen it from them (usually the songs ultimately turn out to have had their roots in a completely different part of the country). "Blue Moon", "Just one of those songs", "Sit Down" and "The Halls of Montezuma" all have both Red and Blue versions, although either the Old Trafford or Maine Road incumbents will claim that they use a song more than the other, and to have a "better" version.

Lower down the Football League, we find that neighbourly antipathy is equally rife, though we were disappointed not to have received any examples of this (or any other songs, for that matter) from Blackpool, Preston or Bolton. It is fair to assume that for the most part, these club's repertoires are made up of the standard North Western songs with the pertinent references altered to reflect the loyalties of the respective supporters.

With regard to the less sensible side of football chanting in the region, the crown rests squarely at Springfield Park, where Wigan's followers have shown a taste for importing soap opera themes from the small screen on to the terraces. Man City made a valiant attempt to come in to the reckoning with their "Banana Splits" effort, but listing the St Winifred's School Choir amongst their influences weighed heavily against them!

Merseyside, and particularly Anfield, proved to be another disappointment with the famed Scouse wit not being too evident in the contributions we had. Liverpool seem to be entirely dependent on just two songs of any length when it comes to intensifying atmosphere, whereas Everton appear to have given up altogether for matches other than derbies. Tranmere have confusingly been allocated to a different geographical area, so their creativity does not come under scrutiny in this particular section.

All in all, this area can reasonably be considered as the country's amost passionate footballing area, and not the North East as is fondly imagined - unless, of course, this rash assertion prompts a landslide of correspondence from Durham and Cleveland to contradict us! (the quality of the songs is, however, not directly proportional to the depth of feeling, better efforts are to be found elsewhere).

110

# BLACKBURN

Another team that have doctored the classic Irish song *"The Wild Rover"*. Having given Burnley's version under their entry, we've first got to wade through the Blackburn Rovers rendition to keep some semblance of parity in this otherwise sadly ill informed publication, see which one you find the more eximious of the two....

"There's an alehouse in Burnley I used to frequent
I met Jimmy Mullen, his money was spent
He asked me to play, and I answered him "Nay!"
'Cos I hate Burnely b\*\*tards 'til my dying day.

And it's, No, Nay, Never, No, Nay Never no more
Will we play Burnley B\*\*tards, no never, no more.

Now I've followed the Rovers for many a year
And I've spent all my money on football and beer
But I've one aim in life before I am gone
That's to follow Blackburn Rovers in Division One

Chorus.....

Now ten years later our team reign supreme
The League and the Cup have been won by our team
And as for Jim Mullen he's now on our side
Because he sweeps the rubbish on our Riverside
And it's No, Nay Never etc.......

More than just a passing similarity with the Turf Moor version! With regard to the relative merits of the two, we have come down firmly on the side of the Burnley variant, if not for lyrical reasons then certainly because any team daft enough to lavish wads of money on a manager whose only claim to fame was to dismantle the half way decent team he inherited at his previous club does not warrant any praise at all (so much for the so called editorial policy of not letting personal bias get in the way of rational writing!). The deep felt antipathy between Blackburn and Burnley is also apparent in this second offering from Ewood Park...(a variation on a much used theme).

"There's a circus in the town (in the town),
Jimmy Mullen is the clown (is the clown),
And Burnley b\*\*tards are in Division Four,
Where we won't see them anymore!"
(Tune: *"There's a tavern in the town"* )

Both the above songs mention Jimmy Mullen who at the time of writing was endeavouring to bring former glories back to Turf Moor as Burnley's manager. Obviously Blackburn's perspicacious supporters will insert the name of the current incumbent when singing either of the aforementioned classics should Mullen's reign end in ignominious failure - unless of course he is replaced by a foreign manager with an extremely long name which doesn't cohere to the existing syncopation and buggers up the flow of the song. Finally, a song which commemorates Rovers' last ditch failure to clinch promotion from the Second Division in 1982 by way of Preston's final-day capitulation to Swansea City, a result which sent the Welsh side up to begin their brief and unsuccessful flirtation with top flight football.

> "On that famous Saturday, the second day of May,
> We met a bunch of Swansea fans on the motorway,
> We said we'd win promotion and we said we'd win the Cup,
> But on that famous Saturday Preston f**ked it up!
> Na, na, na, na, na, na, na, na".
> (Tune: *"John Brown's Body"* )

The references to that particular day as being "famous" is rather mystifying - surely it should be regarded as infamous? Unless of course the Rovers' fans think that missing promotion is cause for celebration, which given that their sadly inadequate team would be taken regularly to the cleaners in Division One, is probably the case.

# BURNLEY

Another one of the currently comatose former giants in the North West, Burnley, like their near neighbours, Blackburn, have adopted "The Wild Rover" as their club song. Having languished for some years in the League's basement, the Turf Moor outfit are currently sweeping towards promotion, so the song will soon be heard in more salubrious surroundings than in recent years, such as, err, Springfield Park and Craven Cottage.....

> "There once was an ale house I used to frequent,
> I saw Ken Dalglish and his money was spent,
> He asked me a question, I answered him"Nay!"
> I said "Rubbish like yours we can beat any day".
>
> And it's No, Nay, Never, No, Nay, Nay Never no more,
> Will we play B**tard Rovers, No never, no more.
>
> Ewood Park is now empty, it's getting knocked down,
> B**tard Rovers play their games on a piece of waste ground,
> With Dalglish on the touchline - say, something's not right,
> There's far more players than supporters in sight,
>
> Chorus
>
> Now five years have passed and Burnley reign supreme,
> The League and the Cup will be won by our team,
> B**tard Rovers are bankrupt and they've long since died,
> And now Ken Dalglish sweeps Burnley's Long Side.

This song apparently first raised the roof of the Long Side during the early seventies, and reflects the intense (and mutual) dislike between the two Lancashire clubs. Recently, it has only been heard at pre season friendlies or at Lancs-Manx Cup ties between the two sides, as Burnley have plummeted down the football league and currently reside two divisions below Dalglish's team.

Blackburn come in for some stick in this next offering too - an altered version of a song derived from one popular with many sets of supporters....

> "One man went to s\*\*t, went to sh\*t on Ewood,
> One man and his dog, Spot, went to sh\*t on Ewood"

.....and so on, presumably up to eleven when the song reaches a suitably rousing climax (to which we are, unfortunately, not party). Burnley's supporters reputedly have a repertoire of some 170 songs, the words to which were distributed prior to a local derby a couple of years ago. We didn't get hold of a copy of this mythical list though, and will have to be content with the songs detailed above, and the following couple of short numbers. John Bond's brief spell in the Turf Moor hot seat (83/84) earned him quite a reputation - he was apparently held solely responsible for the club's decline then, and in years to come, as a result of some mystifying transfer deals. To this day the vast bowl which is Turf Moor echoes to the strains of

> "We hate John Bond and we hate John Bond,
> We hate John Bond and we hate John Bond,
> We hate John Bond and we hate John Bond,
> We are the John Bond HATERS!"

.......seven years on and Bond is still a much hated figure!

On a lighter note, and in common with many other clubs, Burnley have a "song" which is used to accompany all manner of deranged leaping about/surging up and down the terraces type goings on, this behaviour being backed by the cry "Um bah bah, um bah bah, um bah bah..." which was lifted from Malcolm Maclarens' *"Double Dutch"* song. (This also inspired Hull City supporters to uncharted heights of songwriting excellence - fumble feverishly to their entry for details....).

# EVERTON

The Toffees are one of the few First Divison clubs from which we have received a reasonable selection of songs - due in no small part to the way in which they revile their neighbours from across Stanley Park. Liverpool inevitably come in for a good deal of abuse by way of several unique songs......

> "We hate Bill Shankley, we hate St John,
> But most of all we hate Big Ron,
> And we'll hang the Kopites one by one,
> On the banks of the Royal Blue Mersey.
> To hell with Liverpool and Rangers too,
> We'll throw them all in the Mersey,

And we'll fight, fight, fight with all our might,
For the lads in the Royal Blue jerseys."

"Big Ron" we assume to be Ron Yeats, the Reds long serving centre half, and St John is obviously the more odious of the ill informed and infantile combo, Saint and Greavsie. The tune to this is loosely based on *"The Halls of Montezuma"*. On a similar theme.....

"There was a famous derby game,
Some four years ago,
When all the Kop was chanting,
"Kenny, Kenny you must go"
But now you've done the double,
And Kenny is your pride,
You two faced Liverpool b\*\*tards,
You're the sh\*te of Meseyside"
(Tune: Something to do with *"We're on the march with Ally's Army"*)

The well known tendency of those on the Kop to relieve themselves without bothering to vacate their spot on the terrace gets a mention in this version of *"If you ever go across the sea to Ireland"*........

"Now there's a team across the Park at Anfield,
Whose players have no ideas at all (ideas at all),
Now they'd be better off playing snakes and ladders,
It's a shame to let them use a brand new ball (a brand new ball),

If you ever go across the Park to Anfield,
If it's only to see the Toffees play (the Toffees play),
Be sure you take your mackintosh and wellies,
Unless you're liable to float away (to float away),

Now, those Kopites will pee on you in the morning,
Those Kopites will pee on you any time of day (time of day).
For those Kopites don't go to see good football,
They only go to swear and drink bad beer (and drink bad beer)."

The last repeat is sung in a long, drawn out crescendo. That's enough Dirty slagging for now - onto a song in praise of the Blues centre forward Fred Pickering, who carved a place in Evertonian hearts with 56 goals in 97 games between 1963 and 1966. This is to the tune of the Beverley Hillbillies song......

"Now come listen to a story about a man called Fred,
He could score goals with his feet and his head,
Then one day whilst playing against the 'Pool,
He slipped past Yeats and scored one so cool.
(Goals, that is, worth two points.)
When that goal went in all the Kop was in despair,
And all the Evertonians threw their hats in the air,
Even John Moores shouted out with glee,

114

"Freddie Pick, you're the man for me".
Fred.....Hail is the king of E F C."

Apologies for any textual inaccuracies in this - these are due entirely to the incomprehensible handwriting of our contributor. On to another song that celebrates a team's F A Cup triumph, on this occasion, the Blues 1966 victory over Sheffield Wednesday.

"It was on a Saturday afternoon,
In the merry month of May,
That we all went to Wembley,
To see the Toffees play.
There was Alex Young, and Gabriel,
And we played in Royal Blue,
We gave the Wednesday two goals start,
And still beat them 3-2".
(Tune; *"The sash my father wore"*)

The second player referred to is Jimmy Gabriel, Everton's wing half (splendid position!) from 1959 until his departure to Southampton shortly after this Cup Final. Lastly, proof that Blues' supporters do not reserve their hatred solely for Liverpool - Manchester United being on the receiving end in this instance.....

"This old man,
He told me,
Bryan Robson's got V D,
With a nick nack, paddy wack,
Give a dog a bone,
Man United, F**k off home!"
(Tune: Traditional nursery rhyme)

# LIVERPOOL

Right, this one'll settle a few arguments, as the strains of this particular ditty can usually be heard when the T V cameras make their weekly pilgrimage to Anfield, and it always prompts comments such as "What the f**k are the Scousers singing?". Now you can read, learn and inwardly digest the words, join in next time you hear it and amaze all your family and friends.....

"Let me tell you the story of a poor boy,
Who was sent far away from his home,
To fight for his King and his Country,
And also the old folks back home,

They put him in a higher division,
Sent him off to a far foreign land,
Where the flies swarm around in their thousands,
And there's nothing to see but the sand,

The battle started next morning,
Under the Arabian sun,
So remember that poor Scouser Tommy,
Who was shot by an old Nazi gun.

As he lay on the battle field dying, dying, dying,
With the blodd gushing out of his head,
As he lay on the battlefield dying, dying, dying,
These are the last words he said:

(This next bit is sung very loudly, and is about the only section that comes over on the telly...)

Oh I am a Liverpudlian,
From the Spion Kop,
I like to sing, I like to shout,
I go there quite a lot, (distinctly poor line in an otherwise impressive song).
I support a team that play in red,
A team that you all know,
At team that we call Liverpool,
To glory we will go.

We've won the League, we've won the Cup,
We've been to Europe too,
We played the Toffees for a laugh,
And left them feeling blue.
('Nother extremely loud bit here - really exciting "Big finish")
1-2, 1-2-3, 1-2-3-4. FIVE-NIL!.
(Tune: something called *Red River Valley,* we think!)

The last line of this song has become sadly redundant (for the most part) while the Reds have been under the stewardship of Graham Souness - with the exception of the routine demolition of Finnish part-timers Kuusysi Lahtii, and even this was tempered by the return leg in Finland where Grobelaar was at his enigmatic best. Apart from this,the response from Liverpool supporters has belied their reputation as having the wittiest, most vocal supporters in the League, with only one other submission being made.....

"Show them the way to go home,
They're tired and they want to go to bed,
'Cause they're only half a football team,
Compared to the boys in Red".

There is of course the famous Liverpool anthem, *"You'll Never Walk Alone",* but as we've heard nothing to the contrary, we can only assume that they sing the well known version with no alterations...

"As you walk through the storm,
Hold your head up high,
And don't be afraid of the dark,

At the end of the storm,
Is a golden sky,
And the sweet silver song of the lark,
Walk on through the wind,
Walk on through the rain,
Though your dreams be tossed and blown.

Walk on, Walk on,
With hope in your hearts,
And you'll never walk alone,
You'll never walk alone."

The last section is then repeated in its entirety, with two claps inserted halfway through each of the four lines giving this final reprise a much more staccato feel.

As you will have noticed there is a dearth of anti-Everton songs in this section, in stark contrast to the wide range of none too complimentary efforts directed at the Reds by their Goodison counterparts. This mirrors the condescending stance prevalent in Nottingham, with both Forest and Liverpool assuming a patronising "You're not worth singing about" attitude towards their neighbours, who are perceived as being less successful. However, in this instance, our extensive research may have let us down as we are fairly sure that Liverpool express their enmity with Everton via some particularly vitriolic vocal offerings during the so called "biggest local derby in British football" (sic). The lack of any such offerings here is expressly down to the tawdry response from Anfield devotees, and nothing to do with any editorial bias (take note Mr Motson).

# MANCHESTER CITY

Right, some splendid controversy here as we wade straight in with the answer to one of football's most vexing questions with the statement (based on concrete fact after months of research) that it was NOT the Moss Side Muppets who were the first to sing the 1930's Rodgers and Hart classic *"Blue Moon"* in a footballing context. Originally recorded by American group The Marcels, and covered by Bob Dylan (from whose version City's lyrics come) amongst others, the song was first brought to the terraces by Crewe Alexandra supporters who had adopted it (albeit in their homely and endearing world of crap crowds and underachievement) some time before it made its debut at City games.

However, it's obvious to all and sundry that it was City's followers who popularised the song and made it their own after its initial airing at Anfield on their return to the first division in August 1989. The song took a while to become the definitive Maine Road anthem simply because few Bluenoses knew all the words - it wasn't until April 1990 that "Electric Blue" was able to set out the complete lyrics, since when it has become one of the game's best known terrace ditties. Anyway, enough of this tedious history lesson and on with the matter in hand...

"Blue Moon, you saw me standing alone,
Without a dream in my heart,
Without a love of my own.

Blue Moon, you knew just what I was there for,
You heard me saying a prayer for,
Someone I could really care for.

Then suddenly they'll appear before me
The only one my arms could ever hold.
I heard someone whisper "Please adore me",
And when I looked my moon had turned to gold.

Blue Moon, now I'm no longer alone,
Without a dream in my heart,
Without a love of my own".

Right, there you are. From our experience, the song isn't performed in its entirety - the first verse being usually the only bit which gets sung, but even this has spawned a couple of offshoots. The Red half of Manchester jumped on the bandwagon and rewrote the lyrics following Howard Kendall's controversial move back to Goodison Park, and after Brian McClair had saved the Rags' blushes with two late goals in the 90/91 derby - admirable sentiments to record, but rather a poor version.....

"Blue Moon, you started singing too soon
You thought you'd beat us three one
Now Howard Kendall has gone".

It wasn't long however before the Bluenoses came back with another effort, revelling in the memory of their 5-1 hammering of United in September 1989 (indicative of the fact that this result is the only noteworthy thing that City have acheived for a long, long time - hence it's the only thing they've got to sing about).

"Blue Moon, you started singing our tune,
You won't be singing for long,
Cos' we still beat you five - one."

Since City supporters have taken it upon themselves to point out - through the letters page of the Manchester Evening News - that United were not the originators of *"Bright side of life"* (not that they ever claimed to be), yet another version has come to light following the revelation that the song (*Blue Moon*) was plagiarised from Crewe....

"Blue Moon, you're always singing alone,
With just a team of old twats,
Without a song of your own".

And that brings the Blue Moon saga bang up to date!

The other phenomenon which has become inextricably linked with City in recent years is, of course, the inflatable banana. What is perhaps a lesser known facet of the craze is that, whilst standing on the terraces with their new toys, the City fans would sing as much of the theme tune from that well known and much loved holiday programme, The Banana Splits, as memory would permit (the song being reintroduced into the public awareness when the Dickies recorded it in the mid eighties). The basic gist of the song was.....

"One banana, two banana, three banana, four,
Five banana, six banana, seven banana more,
Tra, la, la, tra, la, la, la,
Tra, la, la, tra, la, la, la,
Four banana, three banana, two banana, one,
All bananas playing in the bright warm sun,
Flipping like a pancake, popping like a cork,
Fleagle, Drooper, Bingo and Snork"
Tra, la, la....." etc

The accuracy of the above is somewhat open to question, as it is extremely difficult to discern the words from our aging copy of the Dickies hundred mile an hour recording. The names in the last line are those of the main characters on the TV show - Fleagle being the short fat one with the firemans helmet, Drooper the spaced out lion and Snork the elephantine creation with the enormous shades who never said anything. We sadly can't remember too much about Bingo, he was probably an early incarnation of Peter Swales wearing a far more credible hairpiece than the current effort.

Inevitably, United come in for a degree of criticism, notably through this next song, the words of which would appear to be unique to City's followers - the tune though is the much used *"Wild Rover"*....

"Old Trafford they say is a wonderful place,
But I know it's really a f**king disgrace,
And as for United, I know they should be,
Shovelling s**t on the Isle of Capri".

Yet another instance where a Mediterranean island makes a completely superfluous appearance, as in "From the banks of the River Irwell to the shores of Sicily", the only relevance being the rhyme. The Irwell/Sicily version of this song is common to both Manchester clubs', the words being for the most part as they appear in our entry for Barnsley, other than the obvious name changes.

The conflicting opinions of differing sets of supporters is then admirably illustrated when one considers City's reworking of *"There's no one quite like Grandma"* by the St Winifred's School Choir....

"John Bond, we love you,
John Bond, we do,
Though you may be far away,
We will follow you,

And on Monday when we're Champions,
We'll look back and say,
There's no one quite like John Bond,
He has helped us on our way".

This can be contrasted with the manner in which Bond is viewed by Burnley supporters - whose opinion we tend to favour.

Now, back to the dim and distant past, and the days when silver polish was still a necessary (if occasional) purchase for the cleaning ladies at Maine Road.....

"In 1962, we fell into Division Two,
The Stretford End cried out aloud,
"It's the end of the Sky Blues!",
Joe Mercer came, we played the game,
We went to Rotherham, we won one nil,
And we were back into Division One.
Since then, we've won the League,
We've won the Cup,
We've played in Europe too (and won!)
And when we win the League this year,
We'll sing this song for you."
(Tune: a complete mystery, even though our contributor
  sang it down the 'phone!)

Not a lot you can say about the above, except that it is rather dated. From the more recent past, though still on the subject of unsuccesful attempts to triumph on the domestic front, a song thought to date originally from the 80/81 F A Cup run.....

"I'm dreaming of a blue Wembley,
Just like the one's I used to know,
With the blue flags flying,
And Scousers dying,
To see the City win the cup"

Although this song anticipated a long awaited repetition of the 1969 cup win, an unfortunate deflection from Tommy Hutchison's sternum saw the trophy stay in London on this occasion. By all accounts, this song is trotted out every time City reach the latter stages of the F A Cup, and therefore warrants inclusion due to its rarity value. It is, of course, based on *"White Christmas".*

Right up to the present day now, and our penultimate City offering comes from their visit to Southampton's oh so inviting away end for a league match early in the 91/92 seson. The Blues were en route to a convincing win, generally taking the piss out of Southampton and making them look even more inept than usual, when the Right Said Fred hit of the day became the latest chart/terrace crossover by way of its amendment to "We're too sexy for the Dell, too sexy for the Dell, too sexy....." etc.

Talking of sexy, Niall Quinn is now apparently fawned over with the use of Manfred

120

Mann's "Mighty Quinn". Knowing City's reliance on the 6'4" Irishman this will probably be their next popular and enduring song, and all sorts of arguments will abound with Oldham, Swindon, Portsmouth, Newcastle, Wigan etc etc as to who were the originators, as seems to be the case with the majority of other popular Mancunian anthems.

# MANCHESTER UNITED

It would have been reasonable to expect that the team with the consistently highest average attendances in the League would have had a wealth of splendid songs for our delectation, and this has in fact, proved to be the case. Quantity does not equal quality, however, and in recent years the standard of singing from the "Red Army" (yes, another set of supporters who have taken up this particularly nauseating chant) has been singularly poor.

Over the last couple of seasons, there have been very few new songs other than the stealing of *"Always look on the bright side of life"* from whoever happen to be the latest claimants to have started it (Fulham seeming the most plausible candidates at present). However, as with Blue Moon and Man City, United have to be acknowledged as the team who have popularised this song - it having become a firm favourite during the 1991 Cup Winners Cup run, particularly in Montpellier. The Rotterdam finale to this Euro jaunt gave us......

> "Drink, drink, wherever you may be,
> We are the drunk and disorderly,
> But we don't give a s**t, and we don't give a f**k,
> 'Cos we came home with the Cup Winners Cup."
> (Tune: *"Lord of the Dance"*)

Towards the end of the season, the two expletives in line three were transposed, and the final line became "We're coming home with the Championship". Whether or not this had any prophetic qualities will be apparent shortly following the publication of this book!

The only other major innovation of late saw the light of day at the home game with West Ham in November '91 - the subject being the tabloid press's latest portion of fictitious drivel with regard to the Hammers' reported menage a trois - *"Knees up Mother Brown"* became a pointed and oft repeated reminder of the circumstances surrounding the story, and of the persons involved therein (note a startling degree of editorial discretion as we avoid naming names!) and was used to particular effect by the supporters seated in United's K Stand in drowning out the visiting Hammers' supporters monstrously long performance of "Billy Bonds' Claret and Blue Army". (This repetitious chant was to provide the inspiration for a subsequent United effort)

The eighties spawned another real favourite following Man City's relegation to the Second Division having lost the last crucial match of the season at home to Luton...

> "City versus Luton was heading for a draw,
> Final Saturday of the season,

It had just turned half past four,
David Pleat sent on his sub,
To see what he could do,
He knocked it in and sent the Blues
Back to Divison Two......."

Being based on *"The Laughing Policeman"*, this song ends with several minutes of hysterical laughter.

Lack of recent invention apart, there's a large number of United songs dating back a few years, the most popular of which has become the definitive anthem of the Red's followers.....

"We are just one of those teams that you see now and then,
We sometimes score six, but we seldom score ten,
We beat 'em at home and we beat 'em away,
We'll kill any bastard that gets in our way.

We are the Pride of all Europe, the Cock of the North,
We hate the Scousers, and Cockneys of course,
We are United, without any doubt,
We are the Manchester boys,
La, la, la, la, la, la, la, la, la, la, la, la,
OOOOOOARGH!"
(Tune: *"Just one of those Songs"*)

This song has only recently been heard regularly in its entirety - for years the bulk of the Stretford End (or "the Library" as it has become known recently) seemed not to know the first verse. The final vitriolic scream has only been added during the last couple of seasons - making it one of several songs throughout the League which end in this sort of crescendo. The song is obviously somewhat elderly - United are hardly a team that are seen "Now and again" these days, given the predilection of ITV's programme planners for a Sunday afternoon out at Old Trafford.

As with Everton, United's less than amicable relationship with Liverpool is well documented, and there are several songs which reinforce this mutual dislike. Some of the less unsavoury are.....

"When I was just a little bitty boy,
My grandmother gave me a wonderful toy,
Hundreds of Scousers tied up with string,
She told me to kick their f**king heads in,
Kick their heads in, kick their heads in,
She told me to kick their f**king heads in".

To the tune of Chuck Berry's *"My ding-a-ling"*, this is an unfortunate throwback to the days when violence was commonplace at United - Liverpool matches, a situation which has now thankfully improved.

There is also a version of a well known song, noteworthy as it is the only variant we've found which extends beyond the usual first verse...

"In your Liverpool slums,
In your Liverpool slums,
You look in the dustbin for something to eat,
You find a dead rat and you think it's a treat,
In your Liverpool slums.

In your Liverpool slums,
In your Liverpool slums,
You speak with an accent exceedingly s**t,
Your ma's on the game and your dad's in the nick,
In your Liverpool slums."
(Tune: *"My Liverpool Home"*)

Many other clubs also use the first part of this, with the necessary changes to make it relevant to whoever they are playing on a particular day. In addition to these two, the Kop anthem *"You'll never walk alone"* is always altered to *"You'll never get a job, sign on, sign on..."* etc, and along with *"Does the Social know you're here?"* these two always make an appearance - as they do when the majority of other sides face Liverpool.

United have long been the target for songs from various clubs about Munich (not that they're whiter than white, with both Heysel and to a far lesser extent Hillsborough being used in retaliatory songs). The usual response to these, or nowadays anything vaguely disparaging about the club is either.....

"We'll never die, we'll never die,
We'll never die, we'll never die,
We'll keep the red flag flying high,
'Cos Man United will never die".

.......or

"For ever and ever, we'll follow the boys,
Of Man United, the Busby Babes,
We'll never be mastered,
By you, by you Cockney (Scouse/Midlands etc) b**tards,
'Cos we are United, the Busby Babes".

One of the few things that United have in common with Glasgow Rangers is the following song.....

"Hello, Hello, we are the Busby Boys,
Hello, Hello, we are the Busby boys,
So if you are a City fan, surrender or you'll die,
We all follow United".

The tune, derived from the American Civil War song *"Marching through Georgia"*, is the same as that used by the Ibrox club for their *"Hello, Hello, we are the Billy Boys...."* song, which obviously has other lyrical differences; these two clubs are however particularly noted for the use of these chants.

Back (an extermely long way back!) to United's glory days of the late sixties, and a rambling number recalling the 1968 European Cup triumph....

"We went down to Wembley one sweet night in May,
The crowd was all happy and singing away,
And when it was over and when it was done,
Benfica were beaten by four goals to one.

The first came from Bobby, he outjumped the rest,
The second it came from wee Georgie Best,
The crowd were all cheering, they roared "United",
And the third goal it came from young Brian Kidd.

The crowd were all calling and shouting for more,
So Bobby obliged by making it four,
That night I'll remember whenever I recall,
Manchester United - the greatest of all".
(Tune: basically the verses of *"The Wild Rover"*)

One of the side from the sixties, Denis Law, was afforded a couple of songs in his honour, the first being to the tune of *"Lily the Pink"* by the Scaffold.

"We'll drink a drink, a drink,
To Denis the King, the King, the King,
'Cos he's the leader of our football team,
He is the greatest centre forward,
That the world has ever seen".

The second is yet another which is loosley based on *"The Wild Rover"*....

"There was a young fisherman from Aberdeen,
Played for his country when he was eighteen,
He lead Man United to victory,
And now he's the king of the Football League,
Denis, Denis Law, King of the Football League".

Next, rather more up to date and a very recent addition to the United portfolio. This has been taken up since the promotion of Leeds to the First Division, complete with their subtle Munich dig (ie standing with arms outstretched like wings singing the theme to the Dam Busters). The tune has had just six words added, but this is now sung at every United game with considerable venom and feeling.....

"We all hate Leeds and Leeds and Leeds,
Leeds and Leeds and Leeds and Leeds,
Leeds and Leeds and Leeds,
We all f**king hate Leeds"

124

This is generally repeated for quite some time.

Plunging once more back into the past, we come across a song especially written for United during the halcyon days of the early Fifties (when all manner of stupidity such as League Titles were the order of the day) which goes under the title of "The United Calypso".......

> "If they're playing in your town,
> Be sure to go to that football ground,
> For if you go there you will see,
> The football taught by Matt Busby,
> Manchester, Manchester, Manchester United,
> The team they call the Busby Babes,
> The team they should have knighted."

These words differ slightly from the original during the few airings which the song gets nowadays - it having become the preserve of United's older supporters (or pissed ones such as Richard Davey from Hastings). Another song common to both of the main Manchester clubs is *Yellow Submarine* - the tune being used to accompany eleven repetitions of *"Number one is Georgie Best"* (or Colin Bell in City's case). The number increases with each consecutive line, up to eleven, inferring the significance which the player in question had to the team(s) during their playing days. United's version has, latterly, included a couple of changes, with Bryan Robson being afforded the number seven shirt, Denis Law the ten, and, perversely, the incomparable Ralph Milne gets the eleven!

Next, one of the game's more pertinent and acutely observed songs, as the name of Liverpool's Ian Rush is inserted into the usual *"Gets the ball and does f**k all"* format. Whereas other variants of this inevitably lead to the player in question scoring against the team who's supporters are baiting him (witness Barnsley and Ronnie Moor), Rush has of course failed to score against United in some twenty three games - long may this splendid state of affairs continue!

Mention of Liverpool brings us to another rambling effort which is again based on *"The Wild Rover"*. The chorus will be known to the majority of you, as it is sung, with the relevant team name inserted, by the followers of almost every club in the Football League (particularly by those who frequent Anfield's Kop). The verses, though, depart sharply from the usual *"Wild Rover"* format.......

> "From the dark snows of Munich back in '58,
> I remember those players who once were so great,
> Their memory, it still lingers on in my mind,
> So I'll follow United to the end of my time.
>
> Chorus...
>
> And it's Man United, Man United F C,
> They're by far the greatest team,
> The world has ever seen.
> (Insert "Chester City", "Accrington Stanley" or "Hamilton Academicals"
> to give a reasonable idea of some of the other derivatives of this)

We fought all our battles in Manchester's name,
So listen, you, b**tards, you'll all die in vain,
Others will rise, and others will fall,
But Man United stay the greatest of all.

Repeat chorus....

It's glory and honour, the Great Man he said,
There's nothing on earth like being a Red,
I'll follow them far and I'll follow them near,
And I'll follow United on whisky and beer.

Repeat chorus.....

With regard to the historical references in this song, '"58" refers to the year of the Munich air crash, and the "Great Man" we assume to be Matt Busby.

A more traditional United song which has been recently updated borrows (all right, steals) the tune of Liverpool's *"Red River Valley"*. Whereas the original referred to the European Cup triumph, the new version rather predictably focuses on the Cup Winners Cup victory of 1991......

"If you ever walk down Warwick Road in Salford,
 Buy a ticket for the cantilever stand,
 So you can go and watch the famous Man United,
 Hammer every other b**tard in the land.
 We've beaten all the Polish and the Frenchmen,
 We've beaten Barcelona, pride of Spain,
 We were there in Rotterdam to see United,
 Become the Pride of Europe once again."

In it's previous incarnation, this song referred to Italians and Germans, but has been altered to reflect the teams beaten *en route* to the Feyenoord Stadium (no mention of Wrexham, though, which we feel should really have been made at some point).

Finally, and in spectacularly boring fashion, we come to the latest craze to have swept through the Reds' followers (*"Bright side of life"* now having become rather dated). Having "bubbled under" in the popularity charts for some time, "Ferguson's Red and White Army" came to the fore as United neared the end of the 91/2 season. This was mainly in response to criticism of the standard of vocal backing the team was receiving, and smacks of taking the easy option from the point view of the much maligned supporters, as it provided a noisy backdrop to games with the minimum of creative effort. It did, however, have it's moments - notably at Bramall Lane in March with a sixty five minute performance (including half time) which no doubt boosted sales of Hacks in Sheffields' newsagent's shops after the game!

# OLDHAM ATHLETIC

Contrary to popular belief, Latics supporters have actually got more songs than just "Come on Oldham", which was sung over and over and over and over again to extremely tedious effect during both the 1990 Cup semi final games against Manchester United. One which has emerged during the course of the current (91/2) season is a fairly standard rendition of "The Red Flag" - "ah ha!" we hear you interject, "Surely Oldham play in blue?", well, fair point, but on the odd occasion that they do turn out in their change kit of all-red (ie at Maine Road and presumably Stamford Bridge), this song is most definitely trotted out.

So, that improves the total number of Oldham songs by 100% to a grand total of two. Amazingly, we have come across yet another Boundary Park aria - one which falls into the category of fawning all over a distant hero - from their halcyon days of tangerine away shirts (1966-72). The man in question is Alan Lawson, the "Iron Man" of the team.....

"There was a half back, a Scottish half back,
And Lawson was his name, and clogging was his game,
He came to Oldham, when Celtic sold him,
And Alan Lawson was his name.

For on the green fields down at Boundary,
There's a melee there, bodies everywhere,
For on these green fields down at Boundary,
Alan Lawson reigns supreme.

And Barry Stobart, and Jimmy Fryatt,
He sent them far away, to the infirmary.
He clogged victorious, he clogged so glorious,
And Alan Lawson was his name".
(Tune: *"Scottish Soldier"* by Andy Stewart)

Lawson made 127 league appearances for Oldham between 1964 and 1969, managing to clog one goal in the process. Evidently, he fell victim to a foul from his own savagely violent repertoire - his career ending prematurely at the age of twenty eight, much to the delight of strikers who had suffered under his studs.

Jimmy Fryatt, as mentioned in the above song, managed to force an abrupt about face by the Oldham faithful following his transfer to the club in February 1970. Having avoided any of Lawson's attempts on his life during his previous incarnation at Stockport County, he scored 40 goals in 76 games for the Latics, and was soon afforded a song of his own. This was written to the tune of of Jimmy Deans' *"Big John"*, and contains such classic lines as "Floated like a butterfly 'n' stung like a bee, and he lead Athletic to Division Three". The song never made it onto the terraces, though, and it's therefore not our place to relate it in full.

# WIGAN ATHLETIC

An interesting selection of songs from Springfield Park - home of the Kentucky Fried Chicken Box stand and one of the League's last grass terraces - few of which have any relevance to football itself. Being in the heart of Rugby League country, the Latics' continually have to fight for newspaper/press coverage against the tide of propaganda relating the latest successes for the Cherry and Whites from Central Park. A good deal of animosity exists between the followers of the two different codes of football - especially from the supporters of the eleven a-side game; a selection of songs follows to illustrate this.....

"Who's up Lindsay's arse, who's up Lindsay's arse?
We all, we all, we all know, all the Council's had a go!"
(Tune: *Knees up Mother Brown*)

This refers to the benevolent attitude taken by the local council to Wigan RLFC and their chairman Alec Lindsay, in so far as the redevelopment of Central Park has received substantial subsidies while Springfield Park declines none too gracefully into dereliction, with not a hint of any Council cash being proffered to help out. Joe Lydon's alleged exhibitionist tendencies also merit a mention, his less than savoury reputation being enhanced by the following (to *Quartermasters Stores*)......

'He's here, he's there, he's flashing everywhere,
Joe Lydon, Joe Lydon"

The general dislike of all things pertaining to the oval ball game is hammered home on a regular basis with the heartfelt chorus "We hate Wigan rugby, we hate Wigan rugby", but this sad preoccupation eventually gives way to (shock horror!) some mentions for football. The traditional Lancashire animosity for one's nearest and dearest is predictably aired with.....

"Build a bonfire, build a bonfire,
Put Bolton on the top,
Put Blackpool in the middle,
And burn the f**king lot".
(Tune: *"Clementine"*)

The other popular North West anthem, *The Wild Rover* (ref. Burnley and Blackburn), again appears at Wigan - though we were not blessed with the words to their arrangement. Use your imagination and insert references to Phil Neal and the Wigan Pop Side where suitable to get some idea of what goes on here. A recent fad with the Latics faithful was one for singing the theme tunes to popular TV soaps, and inserting the names of certain characters into football songs, witness......

"Alan Bradley is a w*nker", "Annie Sugden is a druggie"
and "Mrs Mangel's Blue and White army".

These seem to have been fairly shortlived in their popularity and have expired in recent seasons. One longstanding favourite, though, is an effort to redress the balance for the abuse given to Alec Lindsay by having a go at the Wigan AFC chairman who is notorious for his supposed frugal use of the club's money when it comes to improving the squad......

     "He's fat, he's round,
     He never spends a pound,
     Bill Kenyon, Bill Kenyon".
     (Tune: the ubiquitous "Peter Ward" effort from Brighton)

The Wigan die-hards then demonstrated their knowledge of farmyard animal noises, and their sharp-eyed ornithological skills. At an away game at Crewe in 1989, having shrewdly noticed that the Alex custodian went under the name of Dean Greygoose, they greeted his place kicks with the superbly idiotic....

     "Wooooaaahhhhh - gobble, gobble, gobble, gobble...etc"

All in all, another splendid illustration of the wealth of songwriting talent which resides in the lower divisions, and all power to the Latic's supporters in their efforts to have soccer adopted as the town's premier sport, in place of the facile pursuit of a strange shaped ball by thirteen brain dead oafs!

# Section Nine

# The Potteries &

# The Marches

1) Crewe Alexandra

2) Hereford United

3) Port Vale

4) Shrewsbury Town

5) Tranmere Rovers

# THE POTTERIES & MARCHES

Two things stand out in this section, firstly the recollection from dim and distant geography lessons of the term "The Marches" for the rather indistinct area between The West Midlands and Wales, and secondly, the emergence of Tom Jones as a major influence on the match day activities of today's football going youth. The figure of many a middle aged womans fantasy (ooh, patronising sexist stuff now!) has been recently cast as the inspiration for impassioned singing in the Potteries. Unfortunately, the rise to prominence of "Delilah" through the efforts of Stoke City came too late for us to dedicate a complete subsection to the club (hence the brief, almost cursory, mention at the foot of Port Vale's entry) but it has now taken it's place among the other truely strange offerings we have come across, and has become one of football commentator's favourite trivia points. The song is performed with the original words intact in their entirety, and is should soon receive the nationwide acclaim it deserves through a Wembley appearance in the Autoglass Trophy final. The response from Burslem was the adoption of "What's new pussycat?" by the Vale Park faithful - and we can only wait in gaping anticipation for "The green, green grass of home" to crop up at one of the country's other grounds in the not too distant future.

Away from the resurection of stunningly irrelevant chart hits of the past, the region in general follows a similarly unusual pattern, with no one song being popular and no regional themes coming to the fore. The other clubs which we have arbitrarily lumped together, though, do have one common factor in that they all have a unique song or two (with the possible exception of Shrewsbury). We were particularly dismayed not to be able to bring you the full, unexpurgated version of the mysterious "prostitute" song from Prenton Park, but hopefully the inclusion of "The Alexandra Special" has made up for this omission in some small way. Dame Kiri te Kanawa's contribution to the Beautiful Game's heritage should also be noted - definately a gap in the market for a collaboration with Mr Jones in the near future - "Kiri and Tom, live from Gay Meadow", very sensible!

# CREWE ALEXANDRA

Not a great deal submitted by the hordes that frequent Gresty Road, but they do have to be given credit for being the originators of *"Blue Moon"* before it was swiped by the plagiarists from Maine Road (who would do well to remember this fact when they start whingeing about United jumping on the '*Bright side of life"* bandwagon). The words are, however, given under the City entry as they have popularised the song since they first sang it in August 1989. We have to go back to February of the same year to find its origins as a terrace anthem, in fact to Edgely Park, Stockport on the 10th, when the visiting Crewe supporters took up Blue Moon during the course of their 1-0 win. We were given no reason as to why this particular song was chosen, but chosen it was and it soon became a firm favourite at Alex away games. This version of events is confirmed in both local and national newspaper reports, most notably in an article by Mike Langley in the Sunday People at the time (Even though we have to accept that, like the rest of the stuff in the Sunday People, this is probably a complete load of b**locks). In addition to being the derivators of Blue Moon, Crewe also have another rather splendid song based around the tune *"Chatanooga Choo Choo"* (due no doubt to the fact that Crewe is inextricably linked with railways).

> "We're riding along on the Alexandra Special,
> (Woo woo, woo woo !!!)
> Just riding along, singing our song,
> The Alexandra! The Alexandra!"

Top quality stuff, and made all the more admirable given that whilst making the "woo woo" noises it is accepted practice to mime the action of pulling the whistle cord (as on an old steam train) in time to the "words". This song, and its totally humiliating associated actions, has proved to be rather an embarrsment to the Crewe fans, a number of whom stare intently at the ground as their colleagues perform it. We feel though that the grandiose stupidity of the song is something to revel in and be proud of! Given the acute ridicule attached to those who do take part in this strange ritual, it is only performed at away games, where the perpetrators are unlikely to be recognised by family or friends. At home, *Blue Moon* is the predominant song - the only other regular occurrence being the "Gresty Clap", which is nothing to do with unseemly diseases picked up from local pedlars of the flesh but is in fact a well known local propensity for politely clapping (a la Edwardian tennis parties) any facet of the game which the crowd find particularly pleasing - whether it's produced by the Alex or by the visiting team.

The last reported offering from Crewe throws up the interesting (!) juxtaposition between Fourth Divison football and Dame Kire te Kanawa, that large lunged purveyor of many a vibrant aria. The connection comes with the pre 1965 penchant at Gresty Road for performing a song called *"Now is the Hour"*, which you may remember was sung by the aforementioned Dame at the closing ceremony of the Commonwealth Games in New Zealand recently due to it being a traditional Maori song (all right, let's be serious, no one is going to remeber this!). Quite what the reason for this strange predilction was is far beyond our comprehension, so we'll have to consign this to the "inexplicable" file - or possibly the "very dull" file!

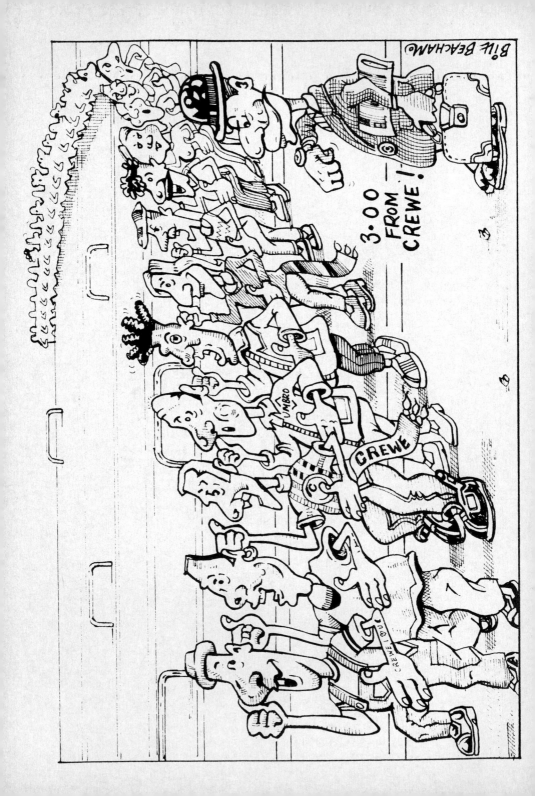

# HEREFORD UNITED

Next to a team who have the eminently sensible attitude of regarding all things Welsh with deep mistrust and an intense dislike - Wrexham in particular. United have the considerable misfortune to have had one of the hideous "Official club songs" thrust upon them, theirs dating from 1979 and being one of the saddest we've come across so far. We're not sure whether or not this has actually made it on the Edgar Street terraces in its original version, if the supporters have any sense of humour it certainly should have. It was recorded by a certain Dave Lee, who our contributor regards as "a pillock who does charity walks from Hereford to Worcester with a pint of beer on his head". We imagine that rather than having the beer balanced in a glass, he has in fact had several pints thrown at him by irate United fans, bent on revenge for the following...

> "Hereford United, we all love you,
> We'll always support you,
> And will follow you through.
> Our supporters are the best and they do their thing,
> When the lads take to the pitch, this is what they sing..."
> (Repeat...)

Er..right..passing swiftly on from that, we come to a song inspired by the club's sponsors - the only such case we're aware of....

> "Kick him in the belly,
> Kick him in the belly,
> Kick him in the belly with a Sun Valley welly, oh yeah!".
> (Tune: *"Beat on the Brat"*, by the Ramones)

Sun Valley are United's benefactors and a local poultry processing company, and their employees (those on the shop floor, anyway) are required to wear wellies under the food hygiene regulations. (While they're at work, not all the time!).

The next song also contains a reference to boots - we're not sure though whether this is another appearance by the Sun Valley wellies or a reference to the ubiquitous Doc Martin. We'll plump for the former, which merits this song's inclusion even though it is really only a variation of a general theme....

> "I was born under the Meadow end,
> I was born under the Meadow End,
> Boots are made for wearing (!),
> Balls are made for kicking,
> And if you are a Wrexham fan,
> We'll kick your f**king head in".

This could have been given a still more prominent regional flavour by changing the fourth line to *"Bulls are made for breeding"* given that sturdy beef cattle are Hereford's most famous export and are often used for cross breeding purposes with Friesian cattle to give a hardy beef/dairy hybrid (not only a book on football songs, but a handy reference work on bovine propagation - what value for money!). This song is of course based on Lee Marvins' *"Wandrin' Star".*

Having tuned into 6.06, Danny Baker's "football" 'phone-in, we can also reveal that the United followers undertake a stirring rendition of the 1976 Peter Shelley classic (!) *"Me and You and a dog named Boo".* The Mr Baker in question will note from the above text that the name of the charity walker which he could not recall during the programme in question is Dave Lee - he would have known this sooner were he to have answered our telephone call!

# PORT VALE

Unsurprisingly, the club who gave football one of its most perplexing fanzine titles - "The Memoirs of Seth Bottomley" - have also conjured up some rather strange songs. The first of these is primarily used at Yuletide fixtures, and is a corruption of *"The twelve days of Christmas".....*

"On the twelfth day of Christmas,
My true love sent to me:
Twelve pints of Bass,
Eleven pints of Bass,
Ten pints of Bass,
Nine pints of Bass,
Eight prints of Bass,
Seven pints of Bass,
Six pints of Bass,
Five Ped-i-grees'
Four pints of Bass,
Three pints of Bass,
Two pints of Bass,
And a pint of Bass in a straight glass...Oooh...Aagh!"

Pedigree is a rather pleasant ale produced by Marston's Breweries, which has recently found its way into Kent, where it has been imbibed to excess by both halves of the Editorial duo who brought you this book - in fact, most of the spelling/grammattical mistakes herein can be attributed to writing whilst under the influence. We thoroughly recommend it.

Our contributor did not state whether the above is sung only in the above format, or if it is performed in its entirety, starting with "On the first day of Christmas....". If the second option is in fact the case, this must be one of the longest songs we have perused, rivalled only by Chelsea's "One man went to Mow", which can go on for some hours.

A less seasonal offering, but nevertheless one with the same admirable attitude to excessive drinking, we have.....

"In a town where I was born,
There's a team we go to see,

136

First we have ten pints of ale (!),
Then we go-o-o,
To see the Vale (SEE THE VALE!),

We all piss in a red and white pot,
A red and white pot, a red and white pot,
We all piss in a red and white pot,
A red and white pot, a red and white pot."
(Tune: *"Yellow Submarine"* )

The *"red and white pot"* is a reference to Stoke City's colours, that other team from the potteries. Although this is a half way decent rendition, it doesn't compare to that done by Marine of the Northern Premier League - full details in our forthcoming (probably years) non-league book. Stoke City come in for more abuse in the following adaptation of the theme tune to *"Selwyn Froggitt"*. The song's prophetic qualities were frighteningly near the mark......

"Stoke are going down, never mind,
Stoke are going down, never mind,
Stoke are going down,
They'll be playing Grimsby Town,
Oh Stoke are going down, never mind,
Oh, never mind."

Stoke did of course go down to the Third Division, but missed an encounter with Grimsby who passed them on the way up - maybe Shrewsbury Town should have been chosen, or are there sinister overtones involved in a fixture versus Grimsby Town that we don't know about?

The vast army that was Port Vales travelling support in the early eighties were notorious for endeavouring to gain admission to the cut-price junior enclosures at the grounds they visited. To facilitate this diabolical fraud, they behaved in a suitably juvenile manner by chanting.....

"Port Vale, Port Vale, Rah, Rah Rah!"

......and also.....

"P-O-R-T V-A-L-E, We like Port Vale, Woo Woo!"

The success, or otherwise, of this deceitful scam is not known to us - any further information gratefully received!

STOP PRESS......It has recently come to light that in response to Stoke City supporters having adopted Tom Jones' *"Delilah"* as their theme tune, Vale Park now echoes to the strains of *"What's new, pussycat?"*. The terraces at the Victoria Ground first rang to *"Delilah"* apparently after it had been heard on the juke box in a pub prior to an unspecified away game - the Vale effort is obviously a straightforward case of jumping on the ever quickening Tom Jones bandwagon! Stoke have also recently taken up strident choruses of "Lou, Lou, Skip to my Lou, Skip to my Lou, Macari", in deferrence to their current manager.

# SHREWSBURY TOWN

From the town more famous for its Flower Festival than any noteworthy footballing achievements (apart from spectacularly removing Wimbledon from the F A Cup in 1991) there comes a selection of some of the strangest songs we've come across. Strange in that a Football League team seems to spend most of its time having a go at supposedly inferior local non league opposition in the shape of Telford United. Anyway, more of this in a while; the first Shrews song we look at has to be this mysterious version of *"Blue Moon"* which has its roots in a local newspaper report on an unsubstantiated incident involving Micky Brown and someone by the name of Brian Clough....

> "Oh, Micky Brown,
> He plays for Shrewsbury Town,
> His favourite group are the Doolies,
> Brian Clough grabbed his goolies".

Very odd indeed, and a story which is perhaps best left uninvestigated. (On the other hand, perhaps it should be vigorously pursued by the gutterpress - maybe it's time that the Almighty Brian got involved in some scandal!).

Now to the first of the rather surreal Telford songs, which, to be wholly fair to our contributor, were supplied with the rider that the name of any other team could be inserted in the appropriate place.....

> "Who's that team they call the Telford,
> Who's that team they all adore,
> And they play in black and white,
> And they are a load of shite,
> And they wont be very happy going home."
> (Tune: *"Ally's army "* )

"Won't be very happy going home" - what is this all about? Has someone at Shrewsbury Central announced that all Telford bound trains are delayed due to leaves on the line or what?

On a different tack, you cannot fault Shrewsbury supporters' passion for fiction - does anyone seriously expect that this following song (popular after a late '70's F A Cup tie) bears any relation to the truth at all...?

> "Chelsea tried, Chelsea died,
> No-one takes the Riverside,
> Na na na na, na na na, na na......" etc

Did the infamous Shrewsbury Headhunters (sic) really give Chelsea a good kicking? - were one of the most infamous hooligan armies in Football history sent fleeing lemming-like into the River Severn, pursued by hordes of rabid Shrews? - we somehow doubt it, unless of course you know different. Next we veer in a somewhat ill structured manner back to the intense local rivalry with Telford United, and Shrewsbury's desire to play in Division Five and taunt the Buck's Head faithfull, to which end they have come up with the following...

"Telford boys, Telford boys,
Nappy rash and Tonka toys."
(To the tune of Sham 69's *"Hersham Boys"*.)

Under John Bond's stewardship, Shrewsbury just might find themselves playing non league football with Telford quicker than they may otherwise have expected, so they really need to come up with some better songs than this if they're going to offend their rivals with any degree of success.

In conclusion, we have a variation on a popular tune which pops up all over the place in one form or another. This particular incarnation however includes one or two lines which are markedly different from the more usual lyrics....

"My old man said follow the Town,
And don't dilly dally on the way,
We"ll take the Station End and all that's in it,
All got your boots on, we'll be there in a minute,
With bottles and spanners, hatchets and spanners,
We don't care what the f**king coppers say,
Cos we are the boys from the Gay, Gay Meadow,
And the kings of football songs,
THE SHREWBURY (clap, clap clap!), THE SHREWSBURY!"

The whereabouts of the mythical Station End is rather contentious, as it doesn't appear to be part of any of the grounds of Shrewsbury's local rivals (unless it's at the Bucks Head, of which we don't have a map!). As to the last line but one, we can only assume that there are a vast selection of songs of which we were not made aware - the absence of which makes this claim appear rather ill founded. Interestingly enough (the readership gasp in expectiation.....!) yet another version of "Don't dilly dally..." appears in the very next section of this book, which may indicate a regional preoccupation with the song on a par with the popularity of "The Wild Rover" in the North West........(it may, of course, do nothing of the sort, but we thought we'd make the point anyway!)

# TRANMERE ROVERS

The renaissance of Tranmere over recent seasons has seen a couple of interesting songs come to light, the first of which unfortunately remains shrouded in mystery, as we have had only sketchy reports of what could be one of the country's classic songs. We would welcome any information which would further our knowledge of this particular effort, which, as far as we can gather is a fairly long winded account of a Tranmere supporter's encounter with a prostitute who has a remarkable collection of tattoos. He is most impressed by the one "just above her fanny, of Al Jolson singing Mammy", splendid stuff indeed!

With that small taster of what will probably turn out to be something completely obscene, we shall move on to a problem which confronts all Rovers supporters - the fact that everyone regards them as Scousers. They are none too happy with this, and have come up with the following to assert their independence from the lesser footballing areas just across the Mersey......

"Don't be mistaken, and don't be mislead,
We're not Scousers, we're from Birkenhead,
You can shove your cathedrals and shove your pierhead,
We all follow Tranmere and that's in Birkenhead".
(Tune: *"The Wild Rover"*)

The last noteworthy contribution from the land of the highly illegal, and not infrequently used, pre-penalty shuffle, falls into the much overused "variations on a theme" category - mildly interesting for the teams named as the opposition to be harmed, the lack of the last two lines and the name of the person or persons to be "followed".....

"My old man said follow the Sheds,
And don't dilly dally on the way,
We took the Wrexham in half a minute,
We took the Chester and the bastards in it,
With bottles and hammers, chisels and spanners,
We're the boys who never run away......"

.....and that's it - no last two lines - no *"So if you are a Wrexham fan, and wearing red and white, then we'll sing F\*\*k off you c\*\*t!"* There is, instead, the cryptic reference to "the Sheds" - who are the less refined members of the Prenton Park assembly who frequent the Cowshed end of the ground. Presumably, before too long, there will be large numbers of new songs singing the praises of a certain goalscoring import/reject from Real Sociadad with an outrageously huge nose - but they'll have to wait for the sequel...!

# Section Ten

# The West Midlands

1) Aston Villa

2) Birminghan City

3) Coventry City

4) West Bromwich Albion

5) Wolverhampton Wanderers

# THE WEST MIDLANDS

The easiest task we've had during the writing of this book is to apportion the title of "singing champions of the West Midlands" to Wolverhampton Wanderers. The unknown quantity of Walsall's fervent following excepted, the quality, amount and standard of chanting at the other grounds in the area is nothing short of appalling. We have tentatively put forward the theory that this may be because of the draconian law enforcement throughout the region, but this is quite clearly a sadly misinformed load of rubbish - so how about some sensible ideas? Well, it could be something to do with the rather paltry attendances at Highfield Road, St Andrews and the rest, but as a number of clubs who are even less well supported have provided us with a far more impressive array of choral offerings, this argument lacks any real weight. An extension of this point (the lack of success factor) is also contradicted by the likes of Crewe Alexandra and Wrexham, so what is the problem with the terrace dwelling songsters from the land of extremely complex motorway interchanges and the Crossroads Motel? After a deal of brow furrowing thought, and a few fairly implausible suggestions, we have surmised that the blame for the lack of Black Country footballing inventiveness must iay fairly and squarely on the shoulders of the publicans of the region. To the best of our knowledge, there is not one decent indigenous pint to be had in the whole West Midlands conurbation, and, with no reasonable source of lubrication for the vocal chords available prior to games, the various groups of supporters are disadvantaged when compared to those who are able to attend matches under the influence of the more interesting beers which can be purchased elsewhere. The West Country's volatile brews, and those which mirror the brooding malevolence of the North East's ales, are obviously far more potent catalysts for vocal extravagance than the insipid offerings from M & B or Banks' (yes, this really is the best we can come up with!).

And so, what of the few songs that are on offer. Apart from Wolves, as previously mentioned, there is really very little to write home about. Birmingham's "Keep right on..." and Coventry's version of the "Eton Boating Song" are the only remotely noteworthy efforts if only from the point of view of their derivations. The St Andrews song is one of the game's most enduring, having persisted since the 1950's, whereas the Cov number apparently sprang up in praise of their new Sky Blue kit which arrived in the late 60's (another of Mr Hill's innovations?). West Brom and Villa, though, are guilty of rather sterile repertoires, which could well do with a bit of inventiveness and, dare we say, humour to brighten them up. The Albion's following do, however, merit some praise for their recently observed end of season ritual which entails attending tha last away game bedecked in fancy dress. We believe the most recent of these outings have involved beachwear, and a toga party at Twerton Park in 1991 - perhaps a few Beach Boys numbers would be appopriate?

# ASTON VILLA

The selection of songs we received from Villa was not commensurate with their standing as one of the country's larger clubs - which just goes to prove our much espoused theory that the quality of a clubs repertoire is not in any way proportional to the size of their support. In fact, "selection" is a complete misnomer for the Villa effort, as it consists of just one song which stands out from the run of the mill ditties attributable to almost every club (see the "general" section for examples of a number of such songs). It dates from some fifteen years ago and refers to the then manager of Birmingham City, whose tenure at St Andrews coincided with a promotional drive from a well known drinks manufacturer.....

> "Willie - Willie - Bell - and - his - c**k - sucking -
> dog - f**king - blue - and - white - homosexual - B**STARDS!!!!!"

This less than wholesome offering is based on the famous "Lip - smacking - thirst - quenching...." etc Pepsi advert which was prevalent in the early to mid seventies, and has few merits other than that it is fairly direct in putting over it's message (ie that Willie Bell and his team were somewhat less than popular at Villa Park). Even the arrival of Ron Atkinson as Villa's manager has failed to inspire any sort of vaguely constructive songwriting - the least we could have expected is that Sammy Davis Juniors' *"Mr Bojangles"* might have become popular amongst the Villans followers! Unfortunately, Big Rons' sudden transferal of allegiance only moved Sheffield Wednesday's supporters to some semblence of creativity - and even this didn't extend beyond the predictable chants of "Judas, Judas" when the teams met at Hillsborough on the opening day of the 91/92 season.

The derisive amount of Villa songs sent in leaves us with some space to fill up, so we will delve into the strange goings on which take place in the Trinity Road on match days and which has earned the supporters therein - and Villa fans generally - the nickname of "Seals" which is widely used in the West Midlands (particularly by West Brom's followers). The patrons who frequent the stand in question - largely a collection of schoolboys and the F.A's much vaunted "family groups" - are given on regular occasions to shriek "Villa, Villa, Villa..." whilst standing on the wooden floor, stamping their feet and clapping with arms extended in front of them. Substitute "Villa" for a suitable barking noise, and imagine a brightly coloured ball balanced on the noses of the perpetrators and you have the perfect performing seal scenario - hence the name. Presumably the picture is completed by the half time refreshment vendors lobbing herring into the crowd as they walk in front of the stand. The only parallel to this sort of percussive behaviour is that of Middlesbrough's Clive Road patrons. (See their entry for full details of this awesomely stupid behavioural abberration).

Whilst "Aston Villa" is not the easiest of names to work into a football song, this is really no excuse for the pathetically limited efforts from the Holte End. However, shocking events were afoot at Anfield for the 6th round F A Cup game (March '92), as the total of notable Villa songs increased by 200% with the advent of the Pompey Chimes tune sung as "Same old Scousers, always cheating" and "........always whingeing". Sour grapes without a doubt, but at least they were original!

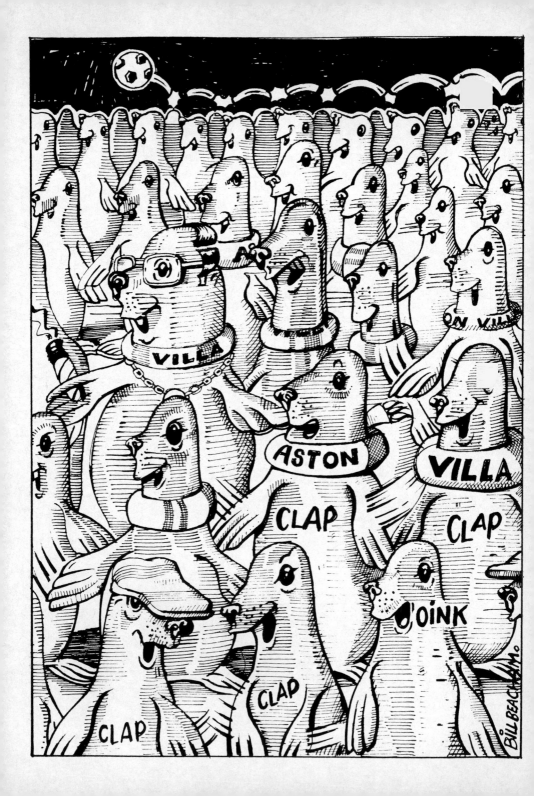

# BIRMINGHAM CITY

The woefully inadequate nature of our contributions from the West Midlands continues apace as we move on to St Andrews. In common with the other clubs in the area, City have a large latent support (witness the recent huge gate for the local derby against West Brom) who have deserted their team rather than stand by them during the fall from the giddy heights of the First Division. Such fecklessness (yeah, all right, I've read "A strange kind of Glory"!) has seen the demise of one of the country's most vocal set of supporters who, in the not too distant past, made the home of the Blues one of the most intimidating of venues for opposing teams to visit through their vocal prowess (this may have also have had something to do with the heyday of the band of delinquents masquerading under the name of "the Zulus" who delighted in chasing visiting fans all over the vast tracts of waste ground surrounding the stadium, not specifically for the purpose of fostering cordial relations with their counterparts from other clubs). The sum of contributions from the second city totalled just one - the following rendition of *"Keep Right on to the End of the Road"* - which, amongst other things provided the title for City's fanzine "Tired and Weary" (see Appendix 1).

> "All through life it's a long, long road,
> There'll be joys and sorrows too,
> As we journey on, we will sing this song,
> For the boys in Royal Blue,
> We're often partisan, la, la, la,
> We will journey on, la ,la, la,
> Keep right on to the end of the road,
> Keep right on to the end.
> Though the way be long,
> Let your hearts be strong,
> Keep right on round the bend,
> Though you're tired and weary,
> Still journey on,
> 'Til you come to your happy abode,
> With all your love,
> We'll be dreaming of,
> We'll be there,
> Where?
> At the end of the road.
> BIRMINGHAM!  BIRMINGHAM!"

It is said by the West Heath Blues that this song was first sung on the team coach by Alex Govan (City's Glaswegian outside left) en route to Wembley in 1956 for the F A Cup final against Manchester City. It was probably performed at the game, too, in celebration of Noel Kinsey's goal (the only high spot in a 1-3 defeat) and would have undoubtedly raised the roof of the famous old stadium had it had one at the time. As far as we know, it has not been sung since, or if it has we can think of no reason why, given Birmingham's inexorable slide down the Football League to third division obscurity, unless of course, the "end of the road" is a euphemism for Division Four!

# COVENTRY CITY

Here we go again (bobbing up and down like this!!!) with another victory for the West Midlands Police in their never ending crusade to remove all trace of enjoyment from watching football. The - how shall we say, earnest? - endeavours of the notorious forces of darkness have succeeded to such an extent at Highfield Road that yet again, a group of supporters who fall regularly under their jurisdiction, have had all the joyous innocence of spectating (metaphorically!) knocked out of them, with the result that vocal support for the Sky Blues is now, to say the least, limited.

Supporters of Jimmy Hill's one time favourite plaything have never been exactly renowned for their vast repertoire of awe inspiring songs, but there is one that you may vaguely recall reverberating around Wembley Stadium on that splendid day in 1987 when Gary Mabbutt was struck suddenly by an irresistible urge to donate the F A Cup to John Sillett's side. This is known as *"The Sky Blue Song"* and is to the tune of the *"Eton Boating Song"*.

> "Let's all sing together,
> Play up Sky Blues,
> While we sing together,
> We will never lose,
> Tottenham or Chelsea,
> United or anyone,
> They can't defeat us,
> We'll fight 'til the game is won".

The song has been trotted out at Highfield Road since it's inception (the song that is) in the 1960's, when the opposing teams named were *"Proud Spurs or Bolton, Wolverhampton or anyone".* The sad demise of all three from the higher sphere of the footballing world (particularly Spurs!) has meant that new sides have been drafted in to suffer a lashing from the rapier wit of the Cov fans. Should the Pride of the Midlands (sic) ever suffer a similar fall from grace, the words will presumably alter to *"Dudley or Bilston, Racing Club Warwick or anyone....."*

Until recently, this was the sum total of vaguely interesting songs which boomed out of the Nicholl Street stand - one season of European football and a single Cup Final appearance not proving to be enough of a catalyst to prompt the City fans into a whirlwind of creativity - however, the 91/92 season, in spite of being singularly unsuccessful, has engendered one other song worthy of note. It is not one of the most inventive efforts we've come across, with the original lyrics retained in their entirety as far as we are aware, so it is an unaltered version of The Beatles *"Twist and Shout"* which inspires the Sky Blues to ever more impressive levels of mediocrity. Why this has been adopted is - surprise, surprise - a complete mystery. There are sadly no songs which sprang up in praise of City's notorious brown kit in the seventies, and a notable lack of vicious assaults on Jimmy Hill - both subjects which were surely deserving of some sort of choral recognition. We can only wait in open mouthed anticipation for the day that Peter Ndlovu finds his name immortalised in song - "We love you, Ndlovu, we do....."?

# WEST BROMWICH ALBION

In spite of having liaised with both the Black Country's answer to David Dimbleby (hello, Chris!) and the Editor of the Albion's leading fanzine (well worth 'phoning up just to hear someone answer with "Hello, Grorty Dick"!) we have come up with only a fairly limited selection of impassioned arias from the Hawthorns. The first three refer to goalscorers who have moved on from West Brom having enjoyed varying degrees of succes during their time at the club. In the first instance, the man in question is Steve Bull who, having scored twice in four appearances for the Albion was transferred to near neighbours Wolves, where he has enjoyed almost God-like status since the move. West Brom's fans are naturally less than pleased at the way things have turned out, and take great pleasure in labelling him a "tatter" every time their paths cross - this being a local derogatory colloquialism for someone akin to Harold Steptoe. The chant itself is nothing more than *"Bully is a tatter, Bully is a tatter, la, la, la, la, OOOH!".* More recently, a genuine Hawthorne's hero was more inventively lauded with....

    "Hark now here the West Brom sing,
    The king is born today,
    His name is Donald Goodman,
    And he's better than Stevie Bull (S**T!!!!)"

Whether or not this is sung only on the 9th of May is the subject of some conjecture, suffice to say that it cetainly won't be on the relevant date this year unless adopted by Sunderland fans.

The last part of this particular trilogy is applicable to Kevin Bartlett, the whippet like striker currently plying his trade at Meadow Lane. Not only did his League registration papers move to Nottinghamshire...so did the basis of a song. The West Brom original differs from the current version only in that instead of being *"Kevin B of Notts County"*, he was *"Kevin B from Cardiff C"* - the free advertising for certain light, chocolatey snacks remained the same in both versions. (Obviously, see the Notts County entry for full details). The structure of this particular chant was evidently a popular one, as it crops up again in this effort directed at journeyman striker (bugger! - for all the above references to "three" and "trilogy", read "four" and "quartet") John Thomas prior to his departure for the permanently greener pastures of Deepdale....

    "Oh Johnny T from Wednesbury,
    Oh Johnny T from Wednesbury,
    Oh Johnny T from Wednesbury,
    He's got a stall on the market,
    Oh Johnny T from Wednesbury".

The story behind the content of this one is that, err, Johnny T comes from Wednesbury, and he's got a stall on the market there (well, that's what we've shrewdly surmised anyway).

Now a few even briefer chants which always make an appearance at Albion games. Firstly there's *"We hate Villa"* and *"We hate seals"*. The Villa version can be heard at any game irrespective of the opposition, while the Seals variant is reserved for when the two teams are in direct confrontation (see Villa's entry for an explanation of the "Seals" tag). Then there's the less than inspiring *"Come on you Baggies"*, notable only as it indicates which one of West Brom's seventeen or so nicknames is the one used by their supporters. *"We love you Oldham, we do"* made an apparently pointless appearance at a West Brom v Bradford game in 1990, pointless that is until you remember that on the same night Oldham were busy dismantling Villa in an F A Cup 6th round tie, something which greatly cheered the West Brom followers who were watching their side in an (ultimately succesful) relegation six pointer.

To finish with, one from the archives, which has not seen the light of day since the mid eighties. It is almost impossible to explain in print - our contributor having been urged to perform it over the phone so we could get some sort of idea as to what goes on. It basically involves the humming of the 1969 Harvey Jay and the Allstars song, *"The Liquidator"*, interspersing a sequence of four claps and a shout of *"West Brom!"* in suitable places. The record was, and possibly still is, played over the P A prior to the Albion's home matches - so if you want to make any sense of what we've written above, we suggest that you make some sort of pilgrimage to the Black Country to take part in the said ritual in person - we're sure it will be worth the effort!

# WOLVERHAMPTON WANDERERS

It's not all that surprising that the biggest response we've had from any of the clubs in the Black Country is that from Wolves, given that anyone sitting in their main stand can't actually see the game in progress and there's nothing left to do but spend 90 minutes making up new songs or occasionally getting rather excited in response to the distant roar which indicates that Steve Bull has scored another goal. There were around fifty songs which we received from Wolves supporters (all courtesy of the excellent "A Load of Bull" fanzine) - there follow a few of the best:

The first is an absolutely majestic version of *"Everywhere we go"* which is sung at virtually every other club in the country as well, but not with quite the same degree of longevity or attention to local detail. As with these other less impressive versions, all the lines are sung twice by differing sections of the crowd - which makes the song even longer...

"Everywhere we go (Everywhere we go)
People want to know (People want to know)
Where the hell are you from? (Where the hell are you from?)
We're from Wolverhampton (We're from Wolverhampton)
Lovely Wolverhampton (Lovely Wolverhampton)
Colourful Wolverhampton (Colourful Wolverhampton)
Buy a corner shop now (Buy a corner shop now)
Selling cheaper lager (Selling cheaper lager)
Tennants' Pilsner (Tennants' Pilsner)
72p a can (72p a can)

Tennants' Extra (Tennants' Extra),
84p a can (84p a can),
Banks' Mild (Banks' Mild),
68p a can (68p a can),

Everywhere we go (Everywhere we go),
People want to know (People want to know),
Where the hell are you from? (Where the hell are you from?),
We're from Wolverhampton (We're from Wolverhampton),
Lovely Wolverhampton (Lovely Wolverhampton),
Colourful Wolverhampton (Colourful Wolverhampton),
Buy a take-away now (Buy a take-away now),
Selling cheaper curry (Selling cheaper curry),
Chicken Madras (Chicken Madras),
Two pounds twenty (Two pounds twenty),
Chicken Vindaloo (Chicken Vindaloo),
Two pounds eighty (Two pounds eighty),
Try a popadom now (Try a popadom now),
42p a piece (42p a piece),

Everywhere we go (Everywhere we go),
People want to know (People want to know),
Where the hell are you from? (Where the hell are you from?),
We're from Wolverhampton (We're from Wolverhampton),
Lovely Wolverhampton (Lovely Wolverhampton),
Colourful Wolverhampton (Colourful Wolverhampton),
Buy a football club now (Buy a football club now),
Call it Wolverhampton (Call it Wolverhampton),
SACK THE BHATTIS! (SACK THE BHATTIS!),
Get promotion (Get promotion),
In the second season (In the second season),
WAN-DER-ERS (clap - clap - clap) WAN-DER-ERS (clap - clap - clap)!"

And that's all there is to it - a simple melody, and a great favourite with Wolves' North Bank choir. These errant songsters have apparently been churning out songs since (history time!) 20th April 1965 during a home game against Sunderland. Prior to this, there were just sporadic chants from the enclosure on the left of the North Bank reserved for schoolboys, but this particular game saw the introduction of organised singing from those at the back of the terrace, and so began a long tradition of Wolves songs.

Another particularly long effort popular at Molineux is an eight verse epic relating the story of Yogi bear (with a couple of diversions into Booboo's alleged bisexuality, his girlfriend's penchent for oral sex and a mention for Ranger Smith) which culminates in Yogi the Wolves fan going on the rampage at Scarborough's first League game and smashing up the ground. Unfortunately, given a lack of time and space, we cannot print this song in full, as there are several other Wolves songs which also merit a mention. One of these should be filed under "Deeply mysterious goings on", as the bloke who sent in the words could think of no other justification for the song being performed other than to "puzzle and bemuse" the visiting supporters and to relieve boredom...

> "Good bye horse, good bye horse,
> He was saying good bye to his horse
> And as he was saying good bye to his horse
> He was saying good bye to his horse".
> (Tune: *"Bless 'em All"*)

This was repeated over and over until everyone got fed up with singing it. However, the song proved to have some value during a game against Leeds, when a section of the visiting support had chosen to view the game from the home terrace. The Wolves fans naturally invited United's followers to leave the area (rather forcibly) and with riot in the air they took up the "Horse" song - the sheer stupidity of which defused the situation with far more effect than any intervention by the West Midland Police could ever have hoped to achieve. Another original from the Wolves choir (who paradoxically now occupy their ground's South Bank), which has been taken up by other supporters up and down the country is:

> "Oh, we do like to be beside the seaside,
> Oh we do like to be beside the sea,
> Oh we do like to walk along the prom, prom, prom,
> Where the brass band plays F**K OFF WEST BROM,
> (and Birmingham)".
> (Tune: Rather obvious!)

The rise to prominence of Steve Bull over recent years has given Wolves fans reason to come up with this little number in adoration of their hero:

> "Hark now hear the South Bank (ah ha!) sing,
> A new king's born today,
> His name is Stevie Bull,
> And he's better than Andy Gray"
> (Tune: Boney M's *"Mary's Boy Child"*)

Finally, back to the seventies, and the only song we've come across yet which is based on a tune by the Monkees (theme to the T V series).

> "Hey hey, we're the Wand'rers
> Waggies on the wing,
> Dougans in the middle
> And Bailey is the king.
> Hey, hey we're the Wand'rers,
> Taylors young we know'
> But he'll be playing for England,
> Down in Mexico".

"Waggie" evidently refers to David Wagstaff, and "Dougan" to Derek Dougan; Taylor and Bailey however, are a bit of a mystery and are the sort of footballing non entities who have contributed to Wolves sad decline in recent years.

# Section Eleven

# Wales and
# The West Country

1) Bristol City

2) Cardiff City

3) Plymouth Argyle

4) Torquay United

5) Wrexham

# WALES & THE WEST COUNTRY

Out on a bit of a limb geographically, this region (or regions) have provided us with several unique songs as befits their relative isolation. To start in England, we have "Drink up thee cider" as performed by Bristol City and, reputedly, Plymouth Argyle. With obvious links to the popular local beverage, this particular ditty hasn't - inspite of it's popularity in the South West - spread to any other part of the country. Home Park has seen the development of a couple of oddities peculiar to the Argyle, the rather strange "Oggie Song" is only to be found there, even though it extols the virtues of Cornish Pasties which are not indigenous to the club's home county of Devon. We also have the "Wembury" chants, which are of course only applicable to the nearest club to this resort. Bristol Rovers much vaunted "Goodnight Irene" is another song exclusive to the area, and is destined to remain a closely guarded secret given Rover's less than forthcoming attitude toward disclosing the lyrics!

As far as Wales is concerned, we were surprised at the lack of any overtly nationalistic songs, given the amount of abuse that the principality and it's inhabitants receive from English clubs. Wrexham's stirring rendition of "Men of Harlech" seems to be the only vaguely defiant song to have cropped up, although Cardiff did make mention of a brief effort glorying in England's dismal European Championship performance of 1988 ("Who put the ball in the England net? Arfur f**king Europe!"). We were less taken aback that the songs of that famous son of the vallies, Tom Jones, had made no impression on the terraces of Ninian Park or the Vetch. These remain the exclusive preserve of the Potteries, and seem as likely to make an appearance in Cymru as do any of Aled Jones's heartfelt arias, although we feel that there should at least be a place for "Walking in the air" during the festive season! Should the much despised Welsh National League ever get off the ground, it would be interesting to note the development of songs performed by supporters of it's participants. Presumably, the glut of local derbies would prompt a number of vehement songs toward new found rivals, although it is perhaps difficult to imagine supporters of the ex Football League clubs being in any way enthusiastic for games under so short sighted a set up.

All in all, there was a rather disappointing response from the region's clubs (the deranged rantings of Plymouth excepted). Perhaps things would improve in line with the fortunes of the clubs, as there seems to be a large floating support for them all (except Torquay and Bristol Rovers) who's attendance at big games would inevitably have a positive effect on the atmosphere. This is, though, no excuse for the lamentable showing of some of them - where were Swansea City? At the very lease, we expected to hear something along the lines of "There's only one Dzemal Hadziabdic", or something glorying in the 12 - 0 destruciton of Sliema Wandererers in 1982!

# BRISTOL CITY

The only club in the West Country with anything halfway decent (Brunel's masterpiece incorporated in their badge and a recent league cup semi appearance) to sing about have, paradoxically, sent in an extremely poor selection of songs. Singing at home games is evidently a thing of the past - the once boisterous Enclosure at Ashton Gate (alternatively called the Chicken Run) has been likened in recent times to *"Clifton Cathedral on the choir's day off"* by City fanzine "The Bountyhunter". Anyone caught singing there these days is looked upon as being one slate short of a watertight roof. Vocal merriment, however still makes a token appearance away from Bristol, there apparently being only one genuine "song" - the ever popular *"Drink up thee Cider"* . This, we presume, is trotted out in both the traditional version, and a new, updated variant devoted to not so local rivals Bristol Rovers since their eviction from Eastville and subsequent tenancy of Twerton Park. First the traditional version..

> "Drink up thee cider, drink up thee cider,
> For tonight we'll merry, merry be,
> We went down the Rovers,
> To do the b**tards over,
> So drink up thee cider in the jar".

...and now the "Tescos Remix"...

> "Drink up thee cider, drink up thee cider,
> For tonight we'll merry, merry be,
> Tesco's went down the Rovers,
> To take old Eastville over,
> And there's no Tote End anymore."
> (Tune: Traditional)

Obviously, this refers to Tesco's having replaced the click of the turnstiles on a Saturday with the squeak of another trolley overloaded with Pampers and disposable Bic razors. The Tote End, prior to becoming the Cold Meats and Dellicatessen counter, was the end of Eastville frequented by Rovers' less savoury supporters. Apart from this, the creativity of City's followers does not extend beyond the odd brief witicism, such as.....

.....when confronted by a less than voluble home crowd at a Leyland Daf game at Reading, the muted Royals fans were told that...

> "You only sing on the toilet, sing on the toilet..."

.....when "on tour" in South Wales (where creativity reaches its peak by the sound of things) on spotting a dog which was in a state of not inconsiderable arousal at Ninian Park:

> "That dog's got a hard on, that dog's got a hard on..."

....and during a subsequent 5-0 demolition of Swansea City at the Vetch Field, all and sundry were informed that...

"The Welsh are f**king shit,
The Welsh are f**king shit,
And now you're gonna believe us....,
The Welsh are f**king shit!"

This match, coincidentally, was also Terry Yorath's first back in charge, after a year long absence, and he came in for some stick as City's goal tally mounted with the satirical.......

"Yorath is back, Yorath is back, hello,
Hello, Yorath is back."

The sentiments towards the Welsh show a complete lack of *entente cordial* between the red shirted citizens of Bristol and their near neighbours from across the Severn estuary. This antipathy, judging by there being no City related abuse from the Welsh clubs, seems to be unreciprocated.

So, not much inventive aplomb in the above, but that's all we received. Even these woefully inadequte submissions, however, are far more impressive than those which were forthcoming from Bristol Rovers. Apart from learning that the Trumpton faithful tend to sing the old music hall favourite *"Goodnight Irene"*, we were given no indication at all as to what is currently in vogue amongst those who wear the quartered blue and white shirts. We are therefore not even going to bother to give them their own section - they'll have to make do with this brief and uncomplimentary addendum to arch rivals City's entry - which should piss 'em off no end. Still, serves 'em right for not bothering to write in!

# CARDIFF CITY

Unlike their Welsh counterparts from the Racecourse Ground, Cardiff have a fairly woeful selection of songs, rather surprising as we would have expected quite a number of efforts regarding the intense local rivalry with Swansea City - one of the few such conflicts of interest which still produces some serious violence on a regular basis. The only contribution we received on this subject was....

"He's a Swansea Jack,
He wears Black and White like he's some sort of queer,
He can't handle women and he can't handle beer,
He's a Swansea Jack."
(Tune: *"My Liverpool Home"*)

Far more impressive was the following in praise of City's goalscoring folk hero, Jimmy Gilligan (35 goals in 97 appearances prior to his £215,000 move to Portsmouth in October 1989). He was evidently viewed as some sort of messiah down at Ninian Park, witness......

154

"God said "Cardiff are the best",
As he spoke to Joseph in his old string vest,
The Virgin Mary said "I've been done,
"Cos I never had a son called Gil-li-gan"

The tune to this second song is somewhat obscure, which is a sadly inadequate way of saying that we don't know it! Other than these, here's just this last effort which commemorates City's 1927 F A Cup win (and also slides in another mention of Swansea at the end)....

"In 1927 in the merry month of May,
The Arsenal went to Wembley,
They walked the Wembley Way.
They thought they'd do the double,
They thought they's lift the Cup,
But along came Cardiff City,
To f**k the b**tards up.

Who's that team they call the Cardiff,
Who's that team they all adore,
We're the boys in Blue and White,
Pissed and looking for a fight,
And we'll hate the Swansea b**tards evermore."
(Tune; *"Glory, Glory Hallelujah"*)

No songs about innovative but unloved club chairman Tony Clemo? - very surprising - and equally so that the Welsh F A don't get any stick for their strange decision to finance floodlights at the Arms Park thereby blowing out Ninian Park as the county's premier football venue - plenty of material there for some really savage songs so we have to conclude that the City faithful could have done better!

# PLYMOUTH ARGYLE

It is reputed that in the fairly recent past Plymouth had a vast selection of songs which were given regular airings up and down the country by the league's most travelled supporters. Things have, however, taken a turn for the worse in more recent times, and we were only able to find brief references to such classics as *"Going up Cambourne Hill"*, *"To be a Pilgrim"* (the John Bunyan hymn), *"You are my sunshine"* and *"Drink up thee cider"* (a la Bristol City) to back up these claims. The words to these ditties were not forthcoming, so we have to make do with the following selection of more modern efforts. In our research for this book, we asked for "songs which you feel are unique to your particular club" from our correspondents, and with this in mind we received these two.......

"Come on you Greens!", and "Green Army, Green Army!"

While these are not especially inventive or interesting, they are certainly unique to Argyle, as they are the only Football League team to play in a predominantly green home strip!

Next, a surprising contribution, in that the first verse is usually sung at West Country supporters in a particularly derogatory way, poking fun at their rural roots and distinctive accents. Argyle's followers have turned this round and adopted it as one of their own songs. It is affectionately known as *"The Oggie Song"* - an "Oggie" being a colloquialism for a cornish pasty.....

> "I can't read and I can't write,
> But that don't really matter,
> 'Cos I come from the West Country,
> And I can drive a tractor.
>
> Oh how happy we shall be,
> To get back to the West Country,
> Where the Oggies grow on trees,
> Oh bugger janner!
>
> And we'll all go back to Oggie land, to Oggie land, to Oggie land,
> Yes, we'll all go back to Oggie land,
> Where you can't tell sugar from tissue paper,
> Tissue paper, marmalade or jam".
> (Tune: Traditional)

Exceedingly strange! And it gets worse.......

> "Ooh ah, ooh ah ah, ooh to be a Southerner,
> Who's that man in the big fat nose?
> The more he eats the more he grows,
> If he eats much more he will explode,
> PLYMOUTH!...PLYMOUTH!...PLYMOUTH!"

This made its first appearance in the early eighties, and persisted on the terraces of grounds where the Argyle faithfull were ensconced until its untimely demise at Dean Court, Bournemouth, in 1986. This song makes a fairly straightforward start before veering off into the realms of complete stupidity. As a matter of some interest "that man IN the big fat nose" is not one of our many textual errors - this is, in fact, what is sung - for whatever reason.

Plymouth's lack of success in major cup competitions has given rise to the next (unsurprisingly) stupid songs - with a couple of subtle differences from a well known and oft used theme......

> "Wembury! Wembury!
> I've got my bucket and spade and I'm of to Wembury"

and.....

> "Wembury! Wembury!
> It's the greatest beach in Devon,
> and its left beside the sea".

Wembury, as opposed to Wembley, is a popular tourist beach near Plymouth, and a far more realistic destination come May for Argyle and the green clad cohorts. The former of the above two is likely to be heard wherever Plymouth play on the first Saturday in January (at home against Oxford United for instance).

Local rivalry is apparently concerned with trying to gain the upper hand over Exeter City (not too difficult a task we imagine), and is illustrated by this next adaptation of *"Knees up Mother Brown"*......

> "City's going down,
> City's going down,
> On the beer we will go.
> Ee aye ee aye ee aye oh!"

As far as we are concerned, this internecine struggle for supremacy is strictly a one horse race, as the residents of the less famous of the two St James' Parks have failed to send us the words to any songs whatsoever. Not a situation which warrants any plaudits in this book - play up, Plymouth and bugger off Exeter! To emphasise how little we think of teams who haven't bothered to write to us, we have little reservation about including the following.....

> "Who's that team they call the Exeter?
> Who's that team team that never score,
> And they play in red and white,
> And they are a load of shite,
> And (the current City manager's) wife is a whore".
> (Tune: *"Glory, Glory, Hallelujah"* )

.....all right, so everybody else sings this as well (with variations) but everybody else's neighbours didn't ignore our polite requests for information, so this seems as good a place to include it as any other. Cannot agree with the last line but they sing it so we wrote it. We understand, that at the time of publication, this was performed in a falsetto, to reflect the voice of the then incumbent boss at St James'!

A special place is reserved in Argyle's folklore for one of their more devoted fans, known to all in Home Park's travelling army as Noddy. Upon the said person's arrival on the visitors terrace he is regaled with the following......

> "Aye oh Noddy, Noddy aye oh!"
> (To the tune of the Pompey chimes)

Also, as Noddy is a legend, the home gathering are ridiculed for not having a figure of equal stature with......

> "We got Noddy, we got Noddy,
> You ain't, you ain't."

Noddy (whoever he may be) apparently has a rather good singing voice and strong West Country burr - Argyle espouse this fact vociferously with.....

"We luuuurrrrvvve yooouuuu Ar-Gal we dooo,
We luuuurrrrvvve yooouuuu Ar-Gal we dooo,
We luuuurrrrvvve yooouuuu Ar-Gal we dooo,
Oh Ar-Gal we luuuurrrrvvve yooouuuu !!."

followed by.....

"Ziiinnnngggg your hearts out for the lads,
Ziiinnnngggg your hearts out for the lads."

The above references to Noddy aptly illustrate the close knit nature of Argyle's small but committed band of travelling songsters, who probably know each other intimately by sight, sound and smell due to their less than awe inspiring number (just how much effort does it take to remember the names of the other four people insane enough to travel away to Newcastle on a Tuesday night to witness a 1-3 defeat?).

# TORQUAY UNITED

One of the League's genuine minnows, United have sent us a proportionately small selection of songs. Evidently uninspired by their last gasp play off triumph which saw promotion to the Third, or by managing to hold Farnborough to a draw at home in the F A Cup, we have to go back to the 1960's to find any sort of vaguely interesting ditties. The first of these was coined in praise of the Gull's all time super hero - Robin Stubbs - who scored a phenomenal total of 121 goals in his 214 appearances for the club over the five years preceding 1968. Evidently some sort of contemporary Errol Flynn adventure saga provided the inspiration.....

"Robin Stubbs, Robin Stubbs, riding through the glen,
Robin Stubbs, Robin Stubbs, with his band of men,
Feared by the bad, loved by the good,
Robin Stubbs, Robin Stubbs, Robin Stubbs".
(Tune: Yet again, the *"Denis More"* thing from Python)

This may have been followed by another verse - perhaps one which mentioned football - but our contributor's powers of recall didn't extend to this.

The other song which caused the very foundations of Plainmoor to tremble in the late sixties followed the award to Torquay of a "Best behaved supporters" title by one of the football magazines of the time. Almost inevitably this gave rise to....

"We're the best behaved supporters in the land,
We're the best behaved supporters in the land,
We're the best behaved supporters,
Best behaved supporters,
Best behaved supporters in the land,
Singing....I threw a bottle at the ref,
I threw a bottle at the ref...." etc.
(Tune: *"She'll be coming round the mountain"* )

This is, we assume, the original which has spawned many a variation in more recent years by other clubs, notably Chelsea. United's adherents have, however, not managed to produce anything else of note since these far off days, which is rather disappointing considering the club's two recent Wembley appearances, which were surely worthy of some sort of expedient vocal efforts. There must be scope for some particulary caustic offerings given the nature of their win over Blackpool in the shadow of the Twin Towers, and even having the smallest ground capacity in the Football League could be used in some sort of song, but the general lack of invention from Devon must lead us to place Torquay in the "could do better" category - still, at least they did better than neighbours Exeter City which may give their supporters some much needed fuel for those beery debates on the respective merits of the two clubs.

# WREXHAM

One of the major surprises we've had in researching this book is the amount of superb songs doing the rounds in the lower divisions. Wrexham's supporters are a prime example of this (as you will shortly be aware) and a favourite pastime on the terraces of the Racecourse seems to be adapting famous national songs to the cause of the Robins, witness this stirring version of *"Men of Harlech"*......

"Here they come our mighty champions,
Raise your voices to the anthem,
Marching like a mighty army,
Wrexham is the name.

See the Reds who fight together,
Speak their names with pride forever,
Marching like a mighty army,
Wrexham is the name.

Fearless in devotion,
Rising to promotion,
To the ranks of mighty heroes.
Fighting foes in every land.
History only tells a story,
We are here to see your glory,
Stand aside, the Reds are coming,
Wrexham is the name.

We have made the mighty humble,
We have made the mountains tumble,
Falling to our mighty army,
Wrexham is the name.

Down the wings the Reds are roaring,
To our greatest goal we're soaring,
Destiny - we hear you calling,
Wrexham is the name."

What can we say - top bollocks song or what? Further stupidity from North Wales is apparent in the following song known as *"It's a lovely old town"* (no idea of the tune here unless this is the title of an actual song).

"I watch my team from the Crispin Lane,
Under the old Bushfield stand,
Dirty old stand, dirty old stand,
In Wrexham town, it's a lovely old town.

Betty the tramp, she lives in a cave,
In Caergwrle, in Caergwrle,
She eats her chips off the King Street floor
In Wrexham town, it's a lovely old town.

We go away in a transit van,
And drink loads of Wrexham lager,
We drink all day and we drink all night,
Then we come home defeated to that lovely old town."

Err...rather odd this one, but a real salt of the earth song of which the public should be aware. The Welsh rugby song *Bread of Heaven* also comes in for some stick by way of...

"Wrexham lager, Wrexham lager,
Feeeeeeed me 'til I want no more (want no more),
Feed me 'til I want no more".

All the usual songs (as detailed in the "general" section of this book) are done, with the butt of most of the abuse being Chester City and in particular their manager Harry McNally, and being in North Wales it was a certainty that *"Day trip to Bangor"* would also be one of the songs submitted (sung exactly as it was performed by Fiddlers Dram!). We can only hope that the genius lyricist who thought up the Reds version of *Men of Harlech* is going strong and churning out many more similar classics (let us know if he is - could be a sequel in the offing here, or at the very least, an edition of "The Official Wrexham F C Songbook").

# Section Twelve

# Scotland &

# Northern Ireland

1) Aberdeen

2) Celtic

3) Heart of Midlothian

4) Kilmarnock

5) Meadowbank Thistle

6) Rangers

7) Cliftonville

8) Glentoran

9) Linfield

# SCOTTISH AND IRISH SECTION

Football supporters both North of the Border and from across the Irish sea have provided a rich source of songs; the Old Firm clubs, Hearts and Meadowbank Thistle being the prime contributors from Scotland, Cliftonville and Glentoran taking the honours in the Emerald Isle. The intensity and passion of songs from these two countries was particularly striking - due in no small part to the way in which religion has become inextricably linked with the Beautiful Game and therefore with the songs of the supporters. We thought long and hard about whether or not to include what can loosely be termed "sectarian" songs, in particular those from Celtic and Rangers, for fear of trivialising a subject which is such an important facet of life both in Glasgow and Northern Ireland. However, the depth of feeling which goes into these songs has made them perhaps the most heartfelt and emotive in Britain, so we have decided to include many of them as no book claming to be the definitive catalogue of terrace songs would be complete should they be excluded. To qualify our actions we have, though, opted to set out only the words to songs from either persuasion which are supportive of the club/beliefs in question - and not to detail any songs which disparrage or abuse the opposing view. There is still a rich selection of songs to review, many of which are traditional and have been transferred to the footballing arena as an afterthought, the national song of the Republic of Ireland having been adopted by Celtic for instance. To further qualify our selection process, we have included songs which are directed at certain clubs and are intended to vilify them on a purely footballing basis. There are, though, a few songs which cross over into the grey area between out and out football chants and the sort of sectarian abuse which we would ideally like to exclude completely. Our understanding of the situation is perhaps not full enough to enable us to differentiate clearly on every occasion between the two, so apologies in advance to anyone who may feel that we have belittled so important a subject by making mention of it - this was never our intention.

On a slightly less contentious point, we should also point out why some of you may find that the words to some of the songs in the Celtic and Rangers sections differ slightly to the version you may know - this is simply because of the huge response we had from both clubs, nearly all of the letters giving differing words for the same songs. It was basically a case of sifting through the pile of letters and editing all the contributions we had, to give the most coherent rendition of each one.

With regard to the limited number of clubs covered in this section, we would point out that songs from the Scottish and Irish game were only included as an afterthought, so we opted to contact only the supporters of those clubs who we felt were likely to have a good selection of songs. Not being experts on either country's terrace singing traditions, we have probably neglected to get in touch with some particularly inventive supporters - so if Albion Rovers, Cowdenbeath or Carrick Rangers fans do claim to have an extensive repertoire of amusing and original chants, perhaps they'd like to write to us and set the record straight. The only supporters who failed to respond to our promptings were those of Berwick Rangers (who we thought may have had some interesting ditties relating to their peculiar position of playing in the Scottish League in spite of being English) - a tad disappointing!

# ABERDEEN

The Dons followers have perhaps surprisingly originated a reasonable selection of songs from the traditional to the downright libellous. In the first category comes the "proper" version of *"The Northern Lights of Old Aberdeen"* (as opposed to the hugely improper version from Tynecastle) which, as well as its more normal rendition has given rise to a splendidly self-deprecatory offshoot....

"When I was a lad, a tiny wee lad,
My mother said to me,
"Go see the Dons, the glorious Dons,
Down at Pittodrie"
They call them the heavenly dancers,
Superb in attack and defence,
I'll never forget that wonderful sight,
I've been a supporter since.

The Northern Lights of Old Aberdeen,
Are home sweet home to me,
The Northern Lights of Old Aberdeen,
Are where I long to be.
I've been a wanderer all of my life,
And many's the sight I've seen.
But God speed the day,
When I'm on my way,
To my home in Old Aberdeen."
(We've got a feeling that this has more than just a passing
similarity to the tune from the *"Finger of Fudge"* advert...)

Now, unlike most supporters, the Dons followers have taken on board the abuse they receive from others in a big way. Rather than responding to the regular assertions that they are fond of a spot of ovine abuse with any equally unpleasent badinage towards the perpetrators, such songs are likely to provoke them only into a strident round of "We f**k sheep", "We're only sheep shagging b**tards" or, splendidly, the club song as detailed above with all the words replaced by "baaah" noises.

Swiftly onwards, and the subject of player worship is a popular one in the Granite City. Former favourites are (or were) greeted with the the following couple of songs.

"There's oniy the one Gordon Strachan,
And he is the king of them all,
When he's on the ball,
We all shout for goal,
'Cos Gordon's the king of them all".
(Tune: *"He's only a poor little sparrow"* or whatever)

"An' then there's Joe Harper, who's King of the North,
He plays at Pittodrie, just up from Kincorth,

He drinks all the whisky and Newcastle Brown,
The Beach End boys are in town.

An' then there's Drew Jarvie, who's bald as a coot,
He knows how to head and he knows how to shoot,
He scores on the ground and he scores in the air,
Who the f**k needs hair?
Drew Jarvie - na, na, na, na, na..." etc
(Tune: would seem to be based on *"The Wild Rover"* )

Lastly on this tack, one in reverence of the famous (!) Danish player, Henning Boel.....

"It's a goal, a goal, a goal for Henning Boel,
It's a goal, it's a goal...."
(Tune: One of many derived from Brighton's *"Peter Ward"* effort)

Nice one, that, just a pity that in one hundred and fifty games for the Dons, Henning found the net just four times, which consigned this song to the "sung down the pub when pissed" category. More frequent, though still to the same tune, is this collection dedicated to Rangers striker Ian Durrant, who was to say the least not overly popular at Pittodrie. The chant evolved to reflect the progression of Durrant's career. From the standard misnomer "He's gay, he's bent, his arse is up for rent" we get "He's gay, he's bent, he's got no ligament" following an injury, which swiftly became "He's gay, he's queer, he's out for a year", adding an element of truth to a clearly misguided chant, when the extent of the damage became clear. The latest amendment arose after an excursion round Glasgow's take-away eateries which ended in a headline making fracas...."He's gay, he's shite, he eats kebabs and fights...". This will obviously run and run to illustrate any such further alleged misfortunes which befall the player in question.

# CELTIC

The Old Firm rivallry is more than just a strictly religious matter. It has transcended this and become a conflict of culture and national identities - Celtic Football Club obviously being a common point around which the Catholic population of Scotland (and elsewhere) can rally to proclaim their independence, and use as a vehicle to assert this. This perhaps explains why so many of the songs from Parkhead are seemingly unrelated to the simplistic world of football. A selection of these so called "rebel songs" follows, the first being *"The Soldiers Song"*, the Irish Republic's anthem....

"We're on the one road, maybe the wrong road,
We're on the road to God knows where,
We're on the one road, maybe the wrong road,
But we're together now, who cares?
North Men, South Men, comrades all,
Soon there'll be no Protestants at all,

We're on the one road, singing a song,
Singing a Soldiers's' Song.

Soldiers are we, who's lives are pledged to Ireland,
Some have come from a land beyond the sea,
Sworn to be free, no more an ancient sire land,
Shall shelter the despot or the slave,
Tonight we'll man the Bar-na-Boile,
In Erin's cause come woe nor weal,
'Midst cannons' roar and rifles' peal,
We will chant a Soldier's Song."

More traditionalism in the form of *"The Merry Ploughboy"*, which contains some farily direct Republican references, and again, ignores football entirely........

"I am a merry ploughboy and I plough the fields by day,
'Til a certain thought came to my mind that I should run away,
Now I've always hated slavery since the day that I was born,
So I'm off to join the I R A and I'm off tomorrow morn'.

Oh, we're all off to Dublin, in the green,
Where our helmets glisten in the sun, F**k the sun,
Where the bayonets flash and the rifles crash,
To the echo of the Thomson gun."

Almost reproduced in its entirety this one - except for a none too complimentary reference to the Queen - the poor old dear gets enough abuse without us chipping in!

This next one is considerably shorter than the previous two, and as such is the exception to the rule with regard to Celtic songs.....

"Roamin' in the gloamin'
With a shamrock in my hand,
Roamin' in the gloamin',
With St Patrick's Fenian band,
And when the music stops,
F**k King Billy and John Knox,
Oh, it's good to be a Roman Catholic."

Lastly, on the historical trip, another epic. We find it hard to believe that these songs are performed as fully unabridged versions, but our contributors assure us that this is the case, so here we go....

"Oh, father, why are you so sad,
On this bright Easter morn?
When Irishmen are proud and glad,
Of the land where they were born.
Oh, son, I see in memory's view,
A far off distant day,

When being just a boy like you,
I joined the I R A.

(Chorus)
Where are the lads that stood with me,
When history was made,
Oh come with me, I long to see,
The boys of the Old Brigade.

On hills and farms, the call to arms,
Was heard by one and all,
And from the glen came brave young men,
To answer Ireland's call,
But long ago, we faced a foe,
The Old Brigade and me,
And by my side, they fought and died,
So Ireland might be free.

(Repeat Chorus)

This is called *"The Boys of the Old Brigade"*, and as with the preceding songs, the tunes are presumably long established as opposed to being relevant to any more modern songs, so unfortunatley we can provide little idea of what they are.

At long last, onto some football related songs, though they still tend to ramble on for hours unlike the more commonplace sort of chanting. This first one harks back to the Coronation Cup of 1953 - the story of which is told in the lyrics....

"Said Lizzie to Phillip as they sat down to dine,
"I've just had a letter from an old friend of mine,
His name is George Young, and he's loyal and true,
And his big broken nose is a light shade of blue."

He says that the Rangers are right on their game,
And they're wanting a trophy to add to their fame,
I'll send up a trophy that Rangers can win",
Said Phillip to Lizzie "Watch the Celts don't step in!".

Said Lizzie to Phillip "They don't stand a chance,
I'll send up the Gunners to lead them a dance,
With Celtic defeated, the way will be clear,
And a cup for the Rangers in my crowning year".

But alas for the hopes of our royal true blues,
The Celts beat the Arsenal, and Manchester too,
With Hibs in the final - a glorious scene,
All Hampden was covered in gold, white and green.

A couple of other verses, which don't seem to be sung as often.....

Said Lizzie to Phillip, when she heard the news,
"A blow has been dealt to my royal true blues,
Please tell me, dear Phillip, for you ought to know,
How to beat Glasgow Celtic and keep them below".

Said Phillip to Lizzie "There's only one way,
And I've known the secret for many a day,
To beat Glasgoww Celtic, you'll have to deport,
All the mad fighting Irish who give them support".

Now for a song which may at last be slightly better known in footballing circles other than Glasgow, as the 91/92 season has seen the advent of the chorus at least making an appearance at a couple of grounds in England - albeit with some minor changes to make it relevant to Man United and Spurs (and, remarkably, Nottingham Forest)....

Starts with the chorus, this one,

"Oh, over and over,
We will follow you,
Over and over,
We will see it through,
We are Celtic supporters,
Faithfull through and through,
And over and over,
We will follow you.

If you go to Germany,
You will see us there,
France or Spain, it's all the same,
We'll go anywhere,
We'll be there to cheer you,
As you travel round,
You can take us anywhere,
We won't let you down.

(Repeat chorus)

If you go to Lisbon,
We'll go once again,
In Zaire, you'll find us there,
Calling out your name,
When you need supporting,
You will always know,
We'll be right there with you,
Everywhere you go."

Lastly, another massively long effort, which, in spite of reputedly being a very popular song, is performed to a tune  which we have been unable to ascertain....

"In the hall of fame, of the football game,
There's a name that stands alone,
It's a Glasgow team, and it reigns supreme,
Where the game of football's known,
For they're good men all, when they're on the ball,
And we know they don't take long,
And the others fear, when they hear us cheer,
As we sing the Celtic song.

(Chorus)

C - E - L - T - I - C, Celtic (see me!),
I see Celtic on the ball,
Each man ready, true and steady,
They'll stand while the others fall,
Shout it proud, like, shout it round, like,
Shout it in the town, like, anywhere at all,
C - E - L - T - I - C, Celtic, I see Celtic,
Celtic on the ball.

When the weeks work's done, and the game's begun,
And as one we cheer the Bhoys,
To the victory that we hope to see,
Then you'll here a brave new noise,
It begins so low, and it starts to grow,
'Til it shakes the football ground,
Then the cheering's out, in a mighty shout,
Of a certain Celtic sound.

(Chorus)

To the football world, there's a challenge hurled,
And it says "Come one, come all",
For we'll watch with pride, as the Celtic side,
They answer to the call,
If  the game is rough, then the Bhoys are tough,
But they always play it clean(!),
For the game's the thing, and the song we sing,
Is the song of white and green."

(Repeat Chorus again)

Hmm....on reflection, the tune for the verses may bear some resemblance to the *"Man United Calypso"*, which is not beyond the bounds of credibility given the links which the two clubs have. The chorus, though, doesn't seem to fit in with any tune that we're aware of - so those of you out there who are not party to the melody will have to experiment and come up with something appropriate.

And that's quite enough Celtic songs! Whether this selection is representative of a standard match day at Parkhead is open to conjecture, as there must surely be a selection of the more usual, shorter songs which are prevalent at other grounds. We were also unable to find the definitive words to one of the less "obscure" songs for which Celtic are known - the one which raises the rafters and begins "Hail, Hail, the Celts are here", before launching into...

"Sure it's a grand old team to play for,
And it's a grand old team to see,
And if...you know...your history,
Then it's enough to make your heart go...ohh...ohh!
We don't care what the Rangers say,
What the hell do they know?
We only know that there's going to be a show,
And the Glasgow Celtic will be there."
(...or something like that!)

There seem - apart from the relgiously aligned ones - to be no songs dirooted at Rangers, which we find rather hard to believe, or at any other Premier League teams. As the repertoires of the majority of other clubs are made up with a good deal of pointed critcism of their opponents, we can only assume that Celtic follow suit even though they were unwilling to impart details of any such goings on.

# HEART OF MIDLOTHIAN

The supporters of Scotland's second or third finest team (depending on the current degree of favour we apportion to Berwick Rangers and Meadowbank Thistle) are responsible for by far the best song other than those associated with the Old Firm (come to that, it's one of the best even including the impassioned ditties from Ibrox and Parkhead). It was written especially for Hearts (or "the Nearly Men of Scottish Football", as they are called by officionados of the game north of the border), by Hector Nicholl during the 1950's. Hector is not known to us for any footballing achievements or for any particular association with Hearts, so the motives behind his creativity remain shrouded in mystery, as do the names of the sea shanties and traditional hymns on which the tune was based. Suffice to say that the hymn from which comes the bulk of the tune was sung during the Eddy Murphy film "Coming to America" by the congregation/audience at the beauty pageant/spiritual gathering - so if you've got a video of the film, you'll soon be able to perform the song, with some alacrity,  should you wish to, in the privacy of your bedroom......

"Away up in Gorgie at Tynecastle Park,
There's a wee fitba' team that'll aye make its mark,
They've won all the honours in footballing arts,
And there's nae other team to compare with the Hearts.

(Chorus)

H - E - A - R - T - S,
If you cannae spell it then here's what it says,
Hearts, Hearts, glorious Hearts,
It's down at Tynecastle they bide,

The talk o' the toon are the Boys in Maroon,
And Auld Reekie supports them with pride.

For national caps we can always supply,
Like Massie and Walker or Bauld and Mackay,
If I had the time I could name dozens more,
Who've helped in producing the old Hampden Roar.

(Chorus)

This is our story, this is our song,
Follow the Hearts and you can't go wrong,
Some say that the Rangers and Celtic are grand,
But the Boys in Maroon are the best in the land.

We've won the League flag and we've won the League Cup,
Though sometimes we go down, we'll aye come back up,
Our forwards can score and it's no idle talk,
Our defence is as strong as the Auld Castle Rock."

This is the offical, unabridged version as sent in by Hearts fanzine, The Jam Piece, but in our experience (the 1986 Scottish Cup Final against Aberdeen) the order of the verses, and one or two of the words, are open to a certain degree of variation. For instance, the last three lines of the chorus are more popularly performed as "It's down at Tynecastle you'll find, the worlds greatest team and their loyal support, who all follow the Jam Tarts with pride", while the last line of verse three appears as "But b**llocks to them, we're the best in the land!" and verses two and four rarley get sung at all.

In addition to this stirring anthem, there are a number of other worthwhile songs from the Tynecastle terraces. The first of these is a particularly splendid version of *"My Way"*, albeit with a traditional chant providing the tune for the last section.....

"And now, the end is near,
We've followed Hearts from Perth to Paisley,
We've travelled far, by bus and car,
And other times, we've gone by railway,
We've been, to Aberdeen, we hate the Hibs,
They make us spew up,
So make a noise, the Gorgie Boys,
Are going to Europe.

To see, H M F C,
We'll even dig your Channel Tunnel,
Or go afloat, on some big boat,
And tie our scarves around the funnel,
We have no fears of other players,
Like Rossi, Boniek or Altobelli,
While overseas, the Hibs'll be
In Porty-belly.

Bring on the Hibs, the Celts, the Rangers,
Bring on Spaniards by the score,
Barcelona, Real Madrid,
They will make a gallant bid,
For they only know the reason why we roar."

This, we believe, was first sung during a game at Pittodrie in October 1989 and obviously refers to Hearts' sorties into Europe, for the most part while intra-city rivals Hibs were languishing at home - ref "In Porty-belly", or Portobello in Edinburgh. It was conceived en route to Prague for what we can only assume to have been a UEFA Cup game, but, whatever the origins, it is certainly one of the finest songs we've received. Still on the subject of European ventures we have......

"Hearts are going to Europe, which no one can deny,
With players like Ferguson, John Colquhoun and Mackay,
Everyone in Gorgie is always on a high,
And Hibs just stayed in Leith, because they couldnae qualify."

Climaxed with a series of "Na na na na na" noises, this would appear to be based on *"The Yellow Rose of Texas".*

Attention then switches away from the much despised Hibernian to a couple of other Premier League protagonists. Firstly, Aberdeen are afforded a corruption of their *"Northern Lights"* song.....

"The Northern Lights of Old Aberdeen,
Mean sweet f**k all to me,
The Northern Lights of Old Aberdeen,
Mean sweet f**k all to me,
I've been a Hearts fan all my life,
And many a sight I've seen,
But the Northern Lights of Old Aberdeen,
Mean sweet f**k all to me."

Next, Rangers, and their inestimable manager came in for some abuse during his time at Ibrox, particularly when details of his wife's dalliance with her Spanish consort came to light in the press. Hearts played Rangers the week after the story broke, with predictable results - notably a song based on a couple of popular chants which first asked *"Souness, where's your wife, Souness, Souness, where's your wife?",* before suggesting a couple of quite feasible, if compromising, places where the lady in question may have been found! Fear of legal retribution unfortunately precludes a more accurate reproduction of the alleged whereabouts of Mrs Souness.......

Further Rangers baiting arose from the signing of Mo Johnstone with all its associated furore....

"Glasgow Rangers, Glasgow Rangers,
You're not fit to wear the Sash,
You're not fit to wear the Sash".

Performed to the *"You're not singing any more...."* tune, this has obvious religious connotations, with "the Sash" being worn by members of Protestant Orange Lodges. The inference being that, having taken a Catholic on board, Rangers had prostituted their Anglican principles and were no longer worthy of their erstwhile traditions.

On a lighter note, the followers of the two Dundee teams have a couple of songs reserved for them. The Blues - when played at Dens Park - are treated to a lusty rendition of the theme to Scooby Doo, in deference to a particular steward who, complete with dated flares, bears a striking resemblance to Shaggy from the said programme. The Tannadice faithful, on the other hand, generally get an earfull of "There's only one United, and that's a f\*\*king biscuit!". Also popular with Man City fans, this asserts that a certain chocolatey comestible is far more impressive than any team with United in their name. Finally, another chant which came in to its own at Hampden Park in 1986. Aimed at Aberdeen - the Scottish equivalent of Leeds - it is sung every time they provide the opposition, but coming from 20000 Hearts fans under the covered end of the famous old stadium, it sounded particularly impressive. It is of course the ubiquitous "Sheep shagging b\*\*tards, you're only sheep shagging b\*\*tards....!"

# KILMARNOCK

From the terraces of the inappropriately named Rugby Park comes an impressive anthology of songs, at which, it has to be said, we were rather surprised. It has been noticeable though, that in researching this book, clubs which have one or two very good fanzines generally also lay claim to a variety of interesting songs - the sort of following that can produce and support succesful fanzines is therefore likely to have a good "songwriting" capacity, with a certain type of humour and inventiveness being common to both phenomena. The ability to improvise and orginate is clear in this reworking of the Rangers song to the tune of *"We're no awa' to bide awa'"* (Definitely the winner of our "extremely strange song title" award).....

> "As I was walking down the Copland Road,
> I met a bunch of strangers,
> They said to me, "Are you going to see
> The famous Glasgow Rangers?"
> So we made our way to Ibrox Park,
> To see my Uncle Willy,
> And the boys in blue got f\*\*ked 6-2,
> By the famous Ayreshire Killie".

Another Rangers song derivitive sees *"The Blue Flag"* get altered, with the second part getting the more radical treatment.....

> "Flying high, up in the sky,
> We'll keep the blue flag flying high,
> Through dirt and muck,
> We'll fight like f\*\*k,
> To keep the blue flag flying high".

On the subject of poaching songs from Souness infected clubs, Liverpool's epic about the soldier (*Red River Valley*) crops up, albeit in as a shortened version....

> "As he lay on the battle field dying,
> With blood pouring out of his head,
> He propped himself up on one elbow,
> And these are the words that he said,
> KILMARNOCK! KILMARNOCK!
> We are the champions!"

Next, and the after match predilection in the blue and white part of Ayrshire appears not to be for the more usual copious amounts of beer, but for a portion of something altogether more interesting....witness this chant full of eager anticipation which was trolled out on the return journey from away matches...

> "If you want a fish supper, clap your hands,
> If you want a fish supper, clap your hands,
> If you want a fish supper, want a fish supper..." etc.

Now, this may be a purely innocent request to the coach driver to stop at the next fish and chip shop he passed to facilitate the purchase of sixpenn'orth of chips and a nice piece of cod, but on the other hand, it could be sung in the hope that on getting home the young ladies with whom the singers consorted would celebrate the Kilmarnock victory in a particularly intimate manner - splendid stuff! (If you've no idea what we're talking about...ask your dad!). Moving swiftly on from any such depravity, we come to what is apparently regarded as a classic which, though short in length, is sung with much vim and vigour...

> "Na, na, na, na, na ,na, hey..ey..ey, Ayrshire Killie!"
> (Another one based on the infamous Bananarama cover)

Still in the "brief" category, we come to one dedicated to fierce local rivals Ayr United, extolling the virtues (or lack thereof) of the main stand at Somerset Park which is of none too rigid construction being made up for the most part from clapboarding (a la Notts County) and chicken wire. The teetering structure apparently sways in the wind, and is lauded with....

> "Who's the clown that built your stand,
> Lego! Lego!
> Who's the clown that built your stand,
> Lego, Legoland!"

Of a more substantial nature (!) is this version of *"Land of Hope and Glory"*, which though popular, is rather contentious when it comes to the correct order of the words - we'll just list 'em and let you arrange them in the most pleasing manner....

> "Land of hope and glory, home of Kilmarnock F C,
> They shall never be beaten...onto victory!
> Men like Jackie McGrory, boys like Tommy McClean
> Here in the West of Scotland, spreading Ayrshire fame".

The last line can also be "We're from the West of Scotland, and we'll bring Ayreshire fame". Equally lines two and four are arbitrarily interchangeable, which arses up the rhyming, and there's yet another line floating around..."They shall never be beaten...onto victory!" to further confuse matters. So, although there's undeniably a well structured and coherent song in there somewhere, we're buggered if we can fathom it out! Finally, a song which is the derivation of the name of one of the aforementioned fanzines.....

"I realise the way your eyes deceive me,
With tender looks that I mistook for love,
So take away the flowers that you gave me,
And send the kind that you remind me of...
Paper roses, paper roses,
Oh how sweet those roses seemed to me,
But they're only imitation,
Like your imitation love for me."
(Tune: believe it or not, *"Paper Roses"*)

And before we are forced to transcribe any more dismal Marie Osmond songs, we will draw a discreet veil over the singing activities at Rugby Park.

# MEADOWBANK THISTLE

Throughout this book a number of groups of supporters - mainly those of so called lesser clubs - have had praise heaped upon them for the way in which they desregard the plight of their team and manage to enjoy themselves by performing a selection of particularly amusing and pointless songs. Well, we now come to the ultimate exponents of this art - the Meadowbank Thistle Brake Club. A group fiercely independent of the official supporters club - for reasons largley beyond our comprehension - the Brake Club have been responsible for the strangest selection of songs ever to have graced football stadia throughout the world, with the possible exception of one heard at certain international fixtures in South America....."Up, down, up, down, f**king hell..... PERU!" Many of these are undoubtedly as a direct result of their (apparent) commitment to get as pissed as possible before, during and after any match they attend, and by way of a response to the taunting they regularly suffer about their team's dismal performances. Anyone who has ever come across the superb and truly seminal fanzine, AWOL, will have a shrewd idea what sort of thing is to follow, as the humour in the stands at "The Concrete Lavvy Pan" (as Meadowbank Stadium is lovingly known) is of much the same ilk as that which made the publication so popular. Not only is the Meadowbank repertoire notable for it's sheer lunacy, but also for it's size - AWOL produced a list of the top one hundred chants used at games! Confronted with such a surfeit of excellence, we'll have to try and categorize the songs if we're to make any sense of things, and we'll start with those culled from television programmes or pop songs. The first is an example of both, as having first been heard on "Chigley", it was later recorded by Half Man Half Biscuit. The words given below are for the version by Liverpool's surrealist songsters, and not those which were used in the programme itself - we're not entirely sure as to which of the two are used by the errant knaves from Meadowbank  Stadium......

174

"Time flies by when you're the driver of a train,
Speeding out of Trumpton with a cargo of cocaine,
Under bridges, over bridges, to our destination,
Careful with that spliff, Eugene, it causes condensation."

Completely irrelevant or what? On a similar tack, both the theme from *"Captain Pugwash"* and that of *"Postman Pat"* have been picked up on. The first is purely an "instrumental", the tune being sung as "Diddley dum, diddly dum, de dum de dum de dum de dum de, diddley dum......" (get the picture?), while the second, somewhat shockingly, bears some relevance to the game itself, with Thistle 'keeper Jim McQueen (a fireman) being lauded with "Fireman Jim, Fireman Jim, Fireman Jim and his Fire Engine". The late seventies British Airways advert was blagged from Celtics' supporters who celebrated a League Championship with "We've won the League again, fly the flag, fly the flag". Thistle, having had a rather less auspicious season finishing bottom of the Second Division, took up "We're bottom of the League, fly the spoon, fly the spoon" - the culinary utensil in question being the metaphorical wooden spoon awarded to Scotland's worst club. Deserving of a verbatim transcription is this next piece of unjustifiable obscenity, to the tune of *"Please release me"*.....

"Please release me, let me go,
For I don't love you anymore,
To live without you'd be a sin,
So release me and let me f**k again,
Oh, f**k again."

Exactly what is the point of this? More easily explicable is this (initially mystifying) version of Stewart and Gaskin's *"It's my party"*...

"Nobody knows where that gas cloud came from,
It's spoiling my view of the game,
I'm wandering around with tears in my eyes,
It's just such a crying shame.
I'm a Hi-bee, and I'll cry if I want to,
Cry if I want to, cry if I want to,
You would cry too if it happened to you."

This is a reference to an incident during an Edinburgh derby (Hibs v Hearts - not one involving Thistle!) when a CS gas canister was lobbed into the midst of the Hibernian support, therby causing much wailing and gnashing of teeth. Many other mainstream songs are also reproduced on the terraces, for the most part in their original format with few alterations. These include: *"I saw a mouse (where? There on the stair)"* ,*"Jolene"*, *"Danny Boy"*, *"Blanket on the Ground"*, *"Crystal Chandelier"*, and Dvorak's *"New World Symphony"*. The last one isn't actually sung as such, but as it's the backing track to the Hovis advert, it is performed whenever one of Thistle's Bradford based supporters makes an appearance.

Second section now - religious hymnals. Only a couple of songs fall into this category, the first being the 23rd Psalm (otherwise known as The Lord's Prayer). This was sung on a visit to one of Lanarkshire's footballing outposts, when the local constabulary were taking a particulary dim view of some of the more obscene chants being aired. Following threats of impending removal from the ground, the Meadowbank contingent stood with hands clasped in prayer, and suitably angelic countenances, intoning "The Lord's my shepherd, I'll not want, he makes me down to lie...." etc. Returning to a more usual style of chant, *"Michael rowed the boat ashore"* was directed at supporters of Clydebank in the form of "Hitler one, Clydebank nil, hallelujah!" - reminding the Kilbowie incumbents of the damage inflicted on their ground by the Luftwaffe during the war. Away from Christendom, the shouts of "Shite, Shite!" which come from opposing fans following a chant of "Thistle, Thistle", are rebuffed with "We're no' Shi-ite, we're the Druze", to *"She'll be coming round the mountain".* This grasp of middle eastern politics is a particular fancy of the Thistle faithful, which is apparently lost on the majority of other supporters throughout the Scottish League - rather unsurprisingly.

Now, for a change, one or two songs which are vaguely related to what might be termed more standard chants. The first two illustrate the popular nickname of the club, which is derived from the less than perfect enunciation of "Thistle". Those without a perfect grasp of the Queens' English (or those with a perfect grasp of the slurring effects on one's speech as caused by several pints of ale) are given to pronounce this as "Fisul". In the first instance, there is a variation on the usual "spelling" chant, where one member of the crowd shouts "Give us an F...give us an I...give us an S..." etc, until, with the help of confederates who supply the letters, the name is spelt out in full and the chant completed by strident shouts of "FISUL!...FISUL!". This was first heard circa 1979, and was popularised by Radio One's John Peel, who often espoused his liking for "Fisul" on his programme (whilst also professing a more questionable allegiance to Liverpool). Secondly, the *"Banana Boat Song"* provides the tune for an altogether stranger chant....

> "Fisul, Fi-i-i-sul, I want a Fisul and I want one now,
> Not one, not two but three goals in it,
> I wanna Fisul and I want one now!"

The less said about this the better. This next song is about as normal as the Thistle following get, as it wouldn't be out of place on the terraces of Tynecastle. Almost inevitably though, the tune is a complete mystery...

> "There is a centre forward,
> Down at Easter Road he plays,
> They say the day that he was born,
> His mother turned away,
> He scores lots of goals,
> Because defenders run away,
> So.....this is what we say:
> STEVIE ARCHIBALD IS UGLY!
> Thank f**k he plays for Hibs".

On further consideration, the tune may bear more than a passing similarity to the much used "Macnamara's Band" - except for the last three lines!

Well, we could go on for several more pages listing all manner of lunacy similar to that detailed above, but chances are it would all get rather boring so we'll wind up with a brief selection of chants which defy being put into categories. The crystal clear atmosphere of the Alps is, in some small way, brought to the terraces of Scotland through performances of the shout which will be well known to avid wachers of Ski Sunday. From a position at the top of a terrace "Hoy! hoy! hoy! hoy! hoy!" is enthusiastically shouted, although we're not sure whether the Thistle following rush headlong down the concrete piste (or pissed!) to add to the realism. Predictably, the merits of drinking are advocated with "We drink beer, we drink wine, we drink meths and turpentine", sung to the tune of Terry Jacks' 1974 hit *"Seasons in the Sun"* - we imagine that in the case of the Brake Club there is more truth in this than may at first be imagined. Lastly, the song which the Thistle fans themselves consider to be their Number One. Including a mention of the one time AWOL editior, "Pastor Milne's Black and Tan Army!" is repeated with feeling for an inordinately long period of time (up to an hour in most cases). The significance of the clerical title afforded to the Brake Club's spiritual leader escapes us, but never the less, this chant has, in the Club's eighteen year senior existence, probably become the most repeated one in the British Isles!

# RANGERS

Rangers supporters have sent in a far more varied selection of songs than their green and white rivals, though there are still quite a few of the "traditional" style songs. Perhaps the best known of these is *"Follow, Follow"*. The structure of the song seems to vary quite considerably - almost all of our many Light Blue contributors sending in a different version. The words, though, remain constant in all these variations - it's the order of the sections which seems rather fluid.....

"Though the straits (or streets) be broad or narrow,
It's follow we will, follow we will,
Though the straits be broad or narrow,
It's follow we will,
We will follow in the footsteps of our team,
God bless them.

Follow, follow, we will follow Rangers,
Anywhere, everywhere, we will follow on,
Dundee, Hamilton, Celtic Park or Hampden,
If they go to Dublin, we will follow on.

There's not a team like the Glasgow Rangers,
No, not one, and there never will be one,
The Celtic know all about their troubles,
We will fight 'til the day is done,
There's not a team like the Glasgow Rangers,
No, not one, and there never will be one.

Follow, follow, we will follow Rangers,
Up the Falls, Derry's Walls, we will follow on,
Follow, follow, we will follow Rangers,
If they go to Dublin, we will follow on."

The second song which is very evident whenever the BBC deign to show us brief highlights of an Old Firm match is the one we have mentioned in the Manchester United section....

"Hello, Hello, we are the Billy Boys,
Hello, Hello, we are the Billy Boys,
We're up to our knees in Fenian blood,
Surrender or you'll die,
For we are the Londonderry Boys."
(Tune: *"Marching Through Georgia"*)

Another popular one kicks off as a shortened version of the Wolves epic *"Everywhere we go"*, before plunging into a rousing climax which is sung at other clubs as a song in its own right....

"Everywhere we go (Everywhere we go),
People want to know (People want to know),
Who the f**king hell we are (Who the f**king hell we are),
Shall we tell them? (Shall we tell them?),
We are the boys in blue and white (We are the boys in blue and white),
We love to sing, we love to fight (We love to sing, we love to fight).

Oh, Oh, Oh Rangers...Rangers,
I'd walk a million miles, for one of your goals,
Oh Rangers".

On to Lee Marvin's contribution to the Ibrox song book, with a corruption of *"Wandrin' Star"* from "Paint your Wagon"...

"Do you know where hell is?
Hell is in the Falls,
Heaven is the Shankhill Road,
And we'll guard old Derry's Walls,
I was born under a Union Jack,
A Union, Union Jack."

This then veers off sharply into the realms of concerted bigotry, so we'll gloss over the second verse and move onto the next song which mentions "old Derry's walls"...possibly because it's called *"Derry's Walls"*......

"Altogether now...the cry was No Surrender,
Surrender or you'll die, die, die,
With heart and hand and sword held high,
We'll guard old Derry's walls.

King James and all his rebel band (censored version!)
Came up to Bishops Gate,
With heart and hand and sword and shield,
We forced them to retreat.

(Chorus)

At last, at last, with one broadside,
Kind heaven sent us aid,
The boom was broke that crossed the Foyle,
And James he was dismayed.

(Chorus)

The banner bright was floated,
That filled our hearts with joy,
God bless the hand that broke the boom,
And saved the Prentice Boys."

There are a few more derivatives from old Protestant battle hymns, the most notable being *"The Sash my father wore"*. It is the chorus only of this lengthy song which is given an airing by the Rangers faithfull....

"It's old and it is beautiful, and it's colours they are fine,
It was worn at Derry, Aughrim, Enniskillen and the Boyne,
My father wore it as a youth, in bygone days of yore,
And it's on the Twelfth I love to wear the sash my father wore."

Next, a portion of *"Here Lies a Soldier"*, though in this case, it's one verse and the chorus which is the popular excerpt....

"Don't bury me in any Fenian valley,
Take me home to Ulster, let me rest,
And on my gravestone, carve this simple message,
"Here lies a soldier of the UVF"

Here lies a soldier, here lies a soldier,
Who fought and died for all he loved the best,
Here lies a soldier, here lies a soldier,
Here lies a soldier of the UVF."

The Paramilitaries also make an appearance in this one...

"Ulster Freedom Fighters we,
Whose cause is life and liberty,
We'll fight and die to keep her free,
We are the sons of Ulster.

So raise the standards, raise them high,
Unfurl the Red Hand, let it fly,
Beneath its colours we'll fight and die,
We'll fight and die for Ulster.

From Derry's ancient city walls,
Armagh, Tyrone, Fermanagh's choice,

With Down and Antrim's men rejoice,
To be the sons of Ulster."

Other older songs to remain in vogue at Ibrox include *"The Old Orange Flute"* - yet another lengthy number that has been considerably altered and shortened for public consumption, *"The Blue Seas of Ibrox"* and *"The Green Grassy slopes of the Boyne"*, but we've devoted enough space to this type of song already and will now move on to chants derived from more commonplace roots.

Firstly, that old favourite *"The Red Flag"*, mutates into *"The Blue Flag"*....

"Wherever we go, we'll fear no foe,
We'll keep the blue flag flying high,
Oh fly it high, up in the sky,
We'll keep the blue flag flying high,
Wherever we go, we'll fear no foe,
We'll keep the blue flag flying high."

This, we think, shares its tune with the *"Ulster Freedom Fighters"* song. Next in line for some severe alterations is *"When the Saints go marching in"*, this being the only substantially different version we've encountered...

"When the Rangers play the Tims,
Oh when the Rangers play the Tims,
I wanna be in that number,
To see another easy win.

When the Rangers start to score,
Oh when the Rangers start to score,
I wanna be in that number,
To sing "The Sash my father wore",

When I hear our battle cry,
Oh when I hear our battle cry,
I wanna be in that number,
To keep the blue flag flying high".

Next, the last of the long winded epics (relief all round)....

"As I was walking down Copland Road, I met a crowd of strangers,
They said to me "Where can we see the famous Glasgow Rangers?",
So I took them off to Ibrox Park, to see a great eleven,
Said I "It isn't Paradise, but man, it's my blue heaven",

Some people write their songs about the land that they adore,
And some of how they fought and won their country's greatest war,
And others still seem quite content to use another theme,
But I've turned out a song about my only favourite team,

For there's no other team in this whole wide world,

From the Real Madrid to the Hotspurs,
Could ever be as dear to me,
As the famous Glasgow Rangers."
(Tune: *"We're no awa' to bide awa'"*)

Again, the Light Blue half of the Old Firm pair have tended towards such interminable ditties such as those detailed above, perhaps to the detriment of the shorter, more spontaneous chants. One which did come to our notice is the singularly short....

"We are the people - we are the people"
(Punctuated by five claps after the words)

Quite what "people" this refers to has escaped the best efforts of our investigative processes, but it makes a change to include a song with something less than seventy four verses. And so, to keep some semblance of balance re: the depth of coverage given, we here draw a veil over the choral machinations of the Ibrox hordes....The End!

# *NORTHERN IRELAND*

## CLIFTONVILLE

Away from the mutual loathing between Glentoran and Linfield, the Red Army from Solitude provided the only other noteworthy contributions from Northern Ireland. Their songs, however, tend to be even more embittered than those from the erstwhile "Big Two", as Cliftonville are one of the few clubs in the area to have a mainly Republican support - the majority of the others in the League being predominantly Loyalist in persuasion. Unlike Celtic, the other great defenders of the faith, the devotees in "The Cage" have shown themselves to be well partial to a bit of complete lunacy through some of their songs - a trait which we find rather admirable. First, though, a selection from the darker side, and the Solitude version of a popular Belfast theme....

"Bless 'em all, bless 'em all,
The long and the short and the tall,
Bless all the forwards and bless all the backs,
Bless all the boys with the red on their backs,
For it's off to Windsor we go - what for?
To give the Linfield a show,
For we'll never be mastered,
By no Orange b*stard,
It's off to Windsor we go!"

Another song prevalent throughout the Smirnoff League is...

"Glory, glory, what a hell of a way to die,
Glory, glory, what a hell of a way to die,

Glory, glory, what a hell of a way to die,
To die an Orange b**tard,
A dirty Orange b**tard."

Though this version is exclusively Cliftonville's, the teams with a Loyalist alignment change "Orange" to "Fenian" to turn the abuse round full circle.

One particular match between Linfield and the Reds saw a very standard chant altered; Cliftonville were 3-0 up at Windsor, heading for an eventual 4-0 win, when "Can you here the Linfield sing?" made a brief appearance. This was swiftly altered to reflect the despair on the faces of the home supporters to...

"Can you see a happy Hun, no-o, no-o,
Can you see a happy Hun, no-o, no-o,
Can you see a happy Hun, I can't see a f**king one...."

..."Hun" being a standard reference to a follower of any mainly Protestant team (especially Rangers in Scottish circles). Still on the sectarian theme, and a startling piece of political awareness from 'Villes supporters aimed at the bulk of Linfields' following in and around the Shankhill Road. This area is represented by a Sinn Fein (Republican) MP, which must piss off the Bluemen quite considerably, and the Red Army feel it their duty to point out this fact by singing *"Gerry Adams is your MP"* several hundred times whenever the teams meet. Our contributor did point out that, conversley, Cliftonville's North Belfast fans are represented by a Unionist, but as yet the Windsor hordes don't seem to have picked up on this and come up with their own biting political comment.

Songs of encouragement for the Reds are of a uniformly standard variety; *"The Red Flag"*, *"Oh, North Belfast is wonderful"*/*"East Belfast is full of shit"*, *"She wore a Red (Scarlet) ribbon"* etc...one or two do stand out though. There is the marvellously succint *"We are Cliftonville.....F**k Linfield!"* (That's it!), and then, from out of the blue, a relative rarity...one of the few songs in the known world which resembles Manchester United's devotional hymn based on the tune *"Just one of those songs"*.....

"We are the Cliftonville, the Pride of the North,
We hate the Glentoran and Linfield of course,
We drink all the cider and sing 'til we're hoarse,
We are the Cliftonville boys."

So, up to this point, an extensive if not amazingly inventive collection, but from here on in things get uniquely surreal. Christmas at the Province's football grounds has been marked in recent years by Cliftonville's followers performing, in it's entirety, *"Feed the world...do they know it's Christmas?"* for some inexplicable reason. Not wholly unique, as Old Trafford occasionally plays host to *"Feed the Scousers...do they know..."*, but this is now augmented by a real one-off. Remember that completely stupid summer hit of 1990, Tim Curry's *"Time Warp"* from the Rocky Horror Picture Show, well, it obviously went down a bundle in North Belfast, as it has become a cult favourite at Solitude.....

"It's just a jump to the left,
And a step to the right,
With your hands on your hips,
You bend your knees in time,
It's just the pelvic thrust,
That drives you insane,
Let's do the Time Warp again..."

Unfortunatley, our chosen medium cannot convey the true grandeur of this, as we assume that all the above actions are carried out in accompaniment to the singing - a genuinely awesome sight. Still not impressed?...well this next one really goes over the top. It was the small collection of Ballyclare Comrades adherents who were the first to witness the crowning glory in the Reds catalogue of idiocy, when the following was belted out during a game between the two teams. Why it was done, we'll probably never know, but nonetheless, it must have provided one of football's most moving scenes, rivalling Doncaster Rovers lunatic fringe in their performance of *"Jerusalem"*.....

"You never close your eyes anymore when I kiss your lips,
There's no tenderness, like before, in your fingertips,
You're trying hard not to show it baby,
But baby, baby, I know it....

You've lost that lovin' feeling, oh that lovin' feeling,
You've lost that lovin' feeling, now it's gone, gone, gone,

Baby, baby, I'd get down on my knees for you,
If you would only love me like you used to do,
We had a love, a love you don't find everyday,
So don't, don't don't let it slip away.

Now there's no tenderness in your arms when I reach for you,
And you're starting to criticise everything I do,
It makes me feel just like crying baby,
'Cos baby, something beautiful's dying.

You've lost that lovin' feeling, oh that lovin' feeling,
You've lost that lovin' feeling, now it's gone, gone, gone."

The above being the Righteous Brothers classic is joined by the even more ludicrous, but equally popular, *"Summer Nights"* and, if this wasn't enough, the tender strains of *"Only fools rush in"* have also been heard echoing from The Cage - to coin another little known chant, *"What the f**k is going on?"*. Any explanation for the advent of these songs really would be very much appreciated - but in the meantime, we must offer our congratulations to the purveyors of such completely ridiculous singing for lending the game it's most splendidly irrelevant musical facet yet!

# GLENTORAN

Even our limited knowledge of football in Northern Ireland has enabled us to detect the less than amicable relationship between the Glens and Linfield, the traditional dislike of any dominant side (ie the residents of Windsor Park) being given added spice by Glentoran being the only side to consistently challenge them for honours in recent years, which has lead to a profusion of big matches between the two clubs. Unsurprisingly, this has lead to the Blues getting more than their fair share of abuse in Glentoran songs such as the following....

All the lines are repeated in this, another (failed) attempt to exceed the inordinate length of the Wolves song....

> "Oh here we go, (Oh here we go),
> We're at it again, (We're at it again),
> We're movin' up (We're movin' up),
> We're movin' in, (We're movin' in),
> We are the lads, (We are the lads),
> From East Belfast, (From East Belfast),
> We are the best, (We are the best),
> So f**k the rest, (So f**k the rest),
> There was a bird, (There was a bird),
> A Linfield bird, (A Linfield bird),
> It landed on, (It landed on),
> My window sill, (My window sill),
> I coaxed it in, (I coaxed it in),
> With a piece of bread, (With a piece of bread),
> And then I crushed, (And then I crushed),
> The birdies head, (The birdies head),
> GLENTORAN!...GLENTORAN!"

More specifically one of Linfields players, Lindsay McKeown, was imortalised on the terraces of the Oval due to his (reputed) extreme ugliness. The Piranhas *"Tom Hark"* was altered to...

> "Lindsay McKeown, the Elephant Man,
> Lindsay McKeown, the Elephant Man,
> Da, da, da, da...OOOH..." etc.

One of the games few terrace dances appeared as a follow up, Glens' fans bouncing around with arms held in a "Play School" style trunk imitating manner whilst chanting *"Let's all do the Lindsay, Let's all do the Lindsay..."*. More short but sweet stuff came to light when Linfield became the proud owners of the only Electronic Scoreboard in the Province. They were evidently more than happy to stuff this fact down the throats of the supporters of other teams, but it became a bit of a liability during the Glens run of seven straight wins over them in 89/90, the visiting supporters drawing attention to the embarrasing scorelines on display with *"Can you see, can you see, can you see your scoreboard now? Can you see your scoreboard now?".*

Movin' on, we come to some standard tunes given a new slant to make them relevant to the Northern Irish soccer scene....

"Forever and ever,
We'll follow the Glens,
Glentoran forever,
We'll follow you,
We'll capture the Gold Cup,
The City Cup too,
If we don't win the League,
The Irish Cup'll do
So let Linfield be b**tards forever!"
(Tune: *"The Red Flag"* )

And (excrutiatingly incorrect way to start a paragraph!) *"Bless 'em all"*, as also used by Cliftonville, gets rehashed too...

"Bless 'em all, bless 'em all,
The long and the short and the tall,
Bless all the forwards,
And half backs and backs,
Bless all the fellows in Red, Green and Black,
For we're singing goodbye to them all,
It's back to the Oval we go,
For we'll not be mastered,
By no Linfield b**tard,
So cheer on the lads, Bless 'em all."

We also received a selection of older, more traditional, songs - along the lines of the Old Firm's rambling efforts. Whether or not these manage to make an appearance on the terraces is somewhat questionable, but here are a couple which look as if they easily could.....

"I am a grand wee Ulsterman,
And Thompson is my name,
I like a drink on Saturday,
I like a football game,
To Windsor Park I like to go,
To see the Blues go down,
'Cos I support Glentoran,
From the other side of town.

I always wear my Glens scarf,
No matter where I go,
I always have it round my neck,
No matter where I've been,
A Blueman tried to strangle me,
He pulled my scarf so tight,
I only said "Come on the Glens",
He wanted me to fight."
(Repeat first section)

This is to the tune of *"The Hills of Donegal"*, and if it is performed at matches, we suspect that the lyrics may well be spiced up a bit with a few obscenities or graphically violent details of the Bluemans fate.

Secondly, and lastly, a lengthy number which reveals that Glentoran possess one of British football's most embarrasing nicknames....

> (Starts with the chorus...)
> "We'll shout at the Oval, we'll shout at the Oval,
> We'll shout "Come on the Glens",
> For there's not another team in the League,
> As good as the wee Cock and Hens (!!!!!!)
>
> If you come to the match and you sit in the stand,
> You come to cheer on the best,
> It's the very best team I've ever seen,
> And I'll tell you, I'm sure you can guess.
>
> (Chorus)
>
> Many a Cup at the Oval we have,
> And I know we'll have many more there,
> So here's to the team we love to support,
> Whose likeness we cannot compare.
>
> (Chorus)
>
> When one of our forwards gets on the ball,
> We let out a deafening roar,
> And if only they'd let us get on the field,
> We'd give them a hand to score.
>
> (Chorus)

This then continues with a litany of famous players to have worn the Red, Green and Black in the past - all of whom seem rather obscure from our vantage point in England, with the exception of "the red haired Dublin boy, Terry Conroy" who went on to set the footballing world alight at Stoke City and Crewe Alexandra - oh, come on, you must remember him!

# LINFIELD

For the most part, Linfield songs are similar to those from Glentoran, except obviously with roles reversed - Linfield being "....the best, so f\*\*k the rest", and the Glens' getting all the abuse. This is not to say that any of the songs were "pinched" from those who attend the Oval and sport the red, black and green, merely that we wrote the Glentoran entry before this one, and there seems little point in reproducing all the songs with only a couple of changes. There are, of course, some songs which do not have a parallel in the Glentoran repertoire, one of these being...

> "Glory, glory, glory, listen to our song,
> We're the Belfast Linfield,
> We're the best team in the land,
> (two, three, four....),
> Bring on the Ballymena,
> Bring on Crusaders too,
> Bring on the shitey Glentoran,
> And we'll show them what to do."

Not at all sure of the tune for that one - it seems to be a conglomeration of about three other chants from throughout the Football League.

The Loyalist connection at Windsor comes through strongly with a number of songs being in common with Glasgow Rangers; *"The Sash", "Follow, Follow", "Old Derry's Walls"* and *"Hello, Hello, we are the Billy boys"* all being favourites of the Linfield followers. Strangely enough, one of the best known Celtic songs has also found its way over the Irish Sea as well, *"Here, here, the Blues are here..."* being the amended introduction to *"Sure, it's a grand old team to play for..."*

Further influence from the mainland is also apparent with the ubiquitous *"Always look on the bright side of life"* being changed to *"Let's all go for a joyride tonight".* This is presumably aimed at the supporters of any Republican teams that the Blues play, the reference obviously being to the large amount of joyriding which takes place in the Province - usually ending in a messy confrontation with the security forces. Equally, however, this may be just a general invitation to anyone to indulge in the passtime, as we're certainly not aware that joyriding is the exclusive preserve of the Republican youth.

Inevitably, there are a couple of more pointed sectarian efforts which make an appearance. There is a particularly vehement reworking of Boney M's *"Holi-Holiday"* about the rapid demise of a number of notable religious figures (that's as specific as we're going to get), and a strange one directed at Glentoran - a "fellow" Protestant team, who nonetheless have a Catholic chapel just down the road from their ground, which lays them open to all sorts of abuse - lack of space and a sudden attack of editiorial discretion however preclude the inclusion of this one too.

# APPENDIX 1

FANZINE TITLES DERIVED FROM SONG TITLES/CHANTS:

As threatened at various points throughout the preceding text, we will now undertake the onerous task of listing all the songs and chants which have provided the inspiration for fanzine titles. This crossover is perhaps indicative of the importance of certain songs to a club's identity - such songs being common rallying points around which supporters can metaphorically gather. The similarity between the mentalities of the songwriting/performing fraternity, and of those people who undertake the production of fanzines has already been touched upon, as has the fact that a club with a rich vein of the said musical inventiveness invariably has an impressive selection of fanzines too. We would not go so far as to say that the terrace Lothario's and the embryonic Hunter Davies's are one and the same, but it would appear that in the vast majority of cases they share the same outlook, opinions and values about the game. The fanzines are continually campaigning for the survival of the very aspects of British football which would ensure the continuance of the all singing/all chanting "subculture" which has provided the material for this book - the retention of the terraces and keeping the game essentially within the fiscal reach of the working classes. Should they fail, and the tide of executive boxes, astronimical admission fees and other television-inspired obscenities fianlly overwhelm the Beautiful Game, then two things would be undeniably poorer - firstly the game itself through the loss of everything which has given it credence and a degree of humanity in the face of the onslaught of the money men, and secondly ourselves, as it would completely bugger up any chance we may have of knocking out a sequel to this book!

Anyway, that's quite enough sociological dissertation from us, on with the matter in hand.....(But first, by way of a rider and to avoid unneccesary repetition, where the relevence of a particular song has escaped us, we've made no comment other than to list the source).....

1) *Only the Lonely* (Airdrieonians) - from the Roy Orbison song of the same title.
2) *Tired and Weary* (Birmingham City) - from their club song "Keep right on to the end of the road". ("Though you're tired and weary, still journey on...").
3) *Here We Go Again!* (Bolton Wanderers) - from the mainly Lancastrian chant "Here we go again, bobbing up and down like this..."
4) *No, Nay, Never* (Burnley) - from "The Wild Rover"
5) *Over and Over* (Celtic) - from the song of the same title "Over and over, we will follow you...."
6) *Glad All Over/ Suffer Little Children* (Crystal Palace) - Now a collaboration between two titles, one obviously from the Palace club song, the other possibly something to do with the Smiths.
7) *Away From the Numbers* (East Fife) - from the Jam song of the same title.
8) *When Skies are Grey* (Everton) - a very common football chant, "....You make me happy, when skies are grey, You'll never know just how much I love you, until you've taken my (........) away." From "You are my sunshine".
9) *Walking Down the Tandragee Road* (Glenavon) - presumably from the Glenavon version of "Blaydon Races".

10) *For Ever and Ever* (Glentoran) - from one of the Oval favourites, "For ever and ever, we'll follow the Glens"

11) *Sing When we're Fishing* (Grimsby Town) - fairly obvious!

12) *No Idle Talk* (Hearts) - from the Hearts Song, "...Our forwards can score and it's no idle talk, our defence is as strong as the Auld Castle Rock..."

13) *Hibees here, Hibees There* (Hibernian) - "....Hibees every f\*\*king where, la, la, la, la, la, la, la,..." etc

14) *Hanging on the Telephone* (Huddersfield Town) - from the Blondie song of the same name.

15) *Those were the Days* (Ipswich Town) - from the Frankie Vaughan / Sandy Shaw song(s) which have proved so confusing throughout this book, "Those were the days, my friend, we thought they'd never end..."

16) *Marching Altogether* (Leeds United) - from their song of the same title..... "Marching altogether, we gonna to see you win...."

17) *One Team in Ulster* (Linfield) - again fairly obvious.

18) *Through the Wind and Rain* (Liverpool) - from "You'll never walk alone".

19) *Show Me The Way To Go Home* (Maidstone United) - from the song of the same title.

20) *Singing the Blues* (Manchester City) - from the song of the same title........ "I never felt more like singing the blues, City win, United lose...."

21) *Fly Me To The Moon* (Middlesbrough) - from "Come fly with me" by Frank Sinatra (among others).

22) *No One Likes Us* (Millwall) - from their definitive chant "...We are Millwall, No one likes us, we don't care..."

23) *The Mighty Quinn* (Newcastle United) - from the much used Manfred Mann track of the same name, in this instance referring to Micky "Carolgees" Quinn late of Portsmouth fame.

24) *What A Load of Cobblers* (Northampton Town) - based on the more usual chant "What a load of rubbish", though with the club's nickname inserted.

25) *Never Mind The Danger* (Norwich City) - from their aged club song, "On the ball, City, Never mind the danger".

26) *Sing When We're Ploughin'* (Norwich City) - Extremely obvious, yet again.

27) *Follow, Follow* (Rangers) - from the interminably repetitive club song of the same name.

28) *Hoops Upside Your Head* (Shamrock Rovers) - from the Gap Band's song of a not disimilar title (Rovers play in green and white hoops).

29) *Cheat!* (Sheffield Wednesday) - from the repetitive and universally known chant used to infer the less than honest behaviour of a player or official who has incurred the wrath of the crowd (ie taking a dive for a penalty, or being the ref who gives such a dubious award).

30) *On the March* (Southampton) - from the 1978 Scotland World Cup number, "We're on the march with Ally's army"

31) *A Love Supreme* (Sunderland) - from the Will Downing song of the same title.

32) *Wise Men Say* (Sunderland) - from that current Roker favourite "Only fools rush in" as recorded by Elvis Presley (again, amongst others).

33) *My Eyes Have Seen The Glory* (Spurs) - from their anthem "John Browns Body / Glory Glory Hallelujah".

34) *Fortune's Always Hiding* (West Ham) - from "I'm forever blowing bubbles" ....."Fortune's always hiding, I've boked everywhere...."

# APPENDIX 2

SONGS WHICH HAVE TRANSFERRED FROM THE CHARTS TO THE TER-
RACES

From the 1960's when the advent of commercial radio made popular music readily accessible to the masses, chart hits have provided the inspriation for a great many terrace songs. From early example such as *"Que Sera Sera"* by Doris Day, and Bing Crosby's *"White Christmas"* to more recent adaptations like *"I'm too sexy...."* by Right Said Fred and James' *"Sit Down"*, Britains footballing public have shown a good deal of invention in altering popular songs to suit their own ends. Below, we have listed all the examples of such plagiarism of which we have been made aware. The song title is followed by the artist (not necessarily the original performer), and then the name(s) of the clubs who have adopted the song. Where a tune is used throughout the league by many clubs, we have named just those who have come up with a substantially different version from the norm (such commonplace chants - shown as being sung by "others" - are also included in the "General" section of the book).

| | | |
|---|---|---|
| A dog named Boo | Pete Shelly | Hereford United |
| A little respect | Erasure | Leyton Orient |
| Annie's Song | John Denver | Sheff United |
| Baby Give it Up | K C & The Sunshine Band | Hull City |
| Banana Boat Song | Harry Belafonte | Meadowbank Thistle |
| | | Sheff United |
| Beat on the Brat | The Ramones | Hereford United |
| Big John | Jimmy Dean | Oldham Athletic |
| Black Betty | The Ram Jam Band | Doncaster Rovers |
| Blanket on the Ground | Billy Jo Spears | Meadowbank Thistle |
| Blue Moon | Bob Dylan | Everyone! |
| Bright Side of Life | Eric Idle | Everyone! |
| Caravan of Love | The Housemartins | Hull City |
| Chatanooga Choo Choo | Glen Miller | Crewe Alexandra |
| Crazy, Crazy Nights. | Kiss | Bradford City |
| Crystal Chandlier | Crystal Gale | Meadowbank Thistle |
| Da do ron ron | Phil Spectre | Bradford City |
| Delilah | Tom Jones | Stoke City |
| Distant Drums | Jim Reeve | York City; Millwall |
| Do they know it's Christmas? | Live Aid | Cliftonville |
| | | Man United |
| Doo wah diddy | Manfred Mann | Leeds United |
| Double Dutch | Malcolm McClaren | Hull City; Burnley |
| Glad All Over | Dave Clark Five | Crystal Palace |
| Hersham Boys | Sham 69 | Shrewsbury Town |
| Hey Girl, don't bother me | The Drifters | Middlesbrough |
| Hi ho silver lining | Jeff Beck | Sheff United |
| | | Sheff Wednesday |
| Holi-holiday | Boney M | Rangers |
| | | Charlton Athletic |

| | | |
|---|---|---|
| I should be so lucky | Kylie Minogue | Reading |
| I'm too sexy | Right Said Fred | Man City |
| Into the valley | The Skids | Charlton Athletic |
| It's my Party | Gaskin / Stewart | Meadowbank Thistle |
| Jolene | Dolly Parton | Meadowbank Thistle |
| Karma Chameleon | Culture Club | Hull City; *et all* |
| Kiss Him Goodbye | Bananarama | Kilmarnock & others |
| Lily the Pink | The Scaffold | Halifax Town |
| | | Manchester United |
| Liquidator | Harvey Jay & The All-stars | West Brom |
| Let's Dance | Chris Montez | Chelsea |
| Mary's Boy Child | Johnny Mathis | West Brom; Wolves; Others |
| Merry Christmas/War is over | John Lennon | Doncaster Rovers |
| Mighty Quinn | Manfred Mann | Portsmouth; Millwall; York City; Hull City; everyone else! |
| Monkees Theme | The Monkees | Wolves |
| Mull of Kintyre | Paul McCartney | Charlton Athletic |
| My ding-a-ling | Chuck Berry | Manchester United |
| My Way | Frank Sinatra | Hearts |
| No-one quite like Grandma | St Winifreds Choir | Man City |
| Only Fools Rush In | Elvis Presley | Sunderland |
| Paper Roses | Marie Osmond | Kilmarnock |
| Peek-a-boo | Siouxsie & Banshees | Chelsea |
| Please Release Me | Engelbert Humperdink | Meadowbank Thistle |
| Prince Charming | Adam & The Ants | Sheff United |
| Sailing | Rod Stewart | Millwall; Maidstone Utd |
| Seasons in the sun | Terry Jacks | Meadowbank Thistle and others |
| Singing the Blues | Frank Isfield | Man City; Reading; Sheff Wednesday |
| Sit Down | James | Man City; Man United |
| Summer Nights | Travolta / Newton-John | Cliftonville |
| Time flies by | Half Man, Half Biscuit | Meadowbank Thistle |
| Time Warp | Tim Curry | Cliftonville |
| Tom Hark | The Piranhas | Glentoran & others |
| Twist & Shout | The Beatles | Coventry City |
| Viva Bobby Joe | The Equals | Southampton |
| We will rock you | Queen | Middlesbrough |
| What's new pussycat? | Tom Jones | Port Vale |
| White Christmas | Bing Crosby | Maidstone; Man City |
| Winter Wonderland | Phil Spectre | Barnet; Reading |
| Wunderbar | Tenpole Tudor | Darlington |
| Yellow Rose of Texas | Dolly Parton | Peterborough;Man City |
| Yellow Submarine | The Beatles | Port Vale; Man City; Reading; Man United; |
| Young, gifted and black | Bob & Marcia | Hull City |
| You've lost that lovin' feelin' | Righteous Brothers | Cliftonville |

# APPENDIX 3

## GENERAL SONGS AND CHANTS COMMON TO MANY CLUBS

At several points in the preceeding text, we've made the sweeping statement that a club's repertoire is made up of "general" chants which are basically used by many other supporters throughout the country. We'll now try to list a few of these, although we cannot hope to include more than a small percentage of the hundreds of short chants which have been used at one time or another. In the following listing, any bracketed names are obviously changed to make a particular song relevant to the game at which it is being sung. As well as brief one or two liners, their are a few slightly longer efforts which tend to crop up regularly, and we'll start with these.

Firstly, The Piranhas "Tom Hark" was used for the basis of this threat to visiting supporters whose team had generally just taken the lead.....

> "You're laughing know, we don't know why,
> 'cos after the match, you're going to die."

This next one is for the most part targetted at television personalities who are commentating on a game (one in particular is often the victim)

> "(Jimmy Hill's) a w**ker, he wears a w**kers hat,
> And when he wears it back to front, He looks a f**king twat."

A particularly popular song has it's roots in the 1978 Scotland World Cup song "We're on the march with Ally's Army" - almost exclusively sung at various cup games - it does, however, occasionally crop up at league matches.....

> "We're on the march with (Cloughie's) Army,
> We're all going to (Wembley),
> And we'll really shake 'em up,
> When we win the (Simod Cup),
> 'cos (Forest) are the greatest football team".

"Mary's Boy Child" is another song to have produced an enduring derivative. The "Boxing Day" reference has now seemingly become almost compulsory, although it may have no specific relevance to any event involving the teams in question....

> "Hark now hear, the (Bolton) sing,
> The (Bury) run away,
> And we will fight for ever more,
> Because of Boxing Day".

Another one aimed at opposing supporters - though seemingly not derived from a named song - is often heard when one of the two followings in attendance is noticeably quieter than their counterparts.....

> "Can you hear the (Carlisle) sing? No-o, no-o,
> Can you hear the (Carlisle) sing? No-o, no-o,
> Can you hear the (Carlisle) sing?
> I can't hear a f**king thing,
> No-o, oh, oh, oh, oh, oh, oh!"

Probably the best known football chant worldwide is Doris Day's *"Que sera, sera"* effort. Spawning many and varied offshoots, the usual format is.....

> "Que sera, sera,
> What ever will be will be,
> We're going to (Wembley),
> Que sera, sera."

Obviously, this is again mainly prevalent at Cup matches, especially when a team finds itself in a winning position in one of the latter-round matches. Perversely, a song which is usually associated with impending success also appears in less auspicious circumstances when a club's supporters acknowledge the inevitability of relegation, with the name of a team in the lower division where the club are bound used in place of "Wembley". Away from these rather longer songs, it's fairly easy to categorize the chants which go to make up the bulk of the selection you can here at any venue in Britain during the course of a game. We'll start with those directed at opposing supporters, whether to threaten, taunt, mock or simply make fun of them. Firstly, there are a few chants which are used to draw attention to the fact that very few people have turned up to support a team - generally aimed at small travelling bands, they may occur should a team's home attendances drop to laughable proportions:

> "Is that all you bring away / get at home?"

> "You must have come in a taxi / on a skateboard"

> "Can you see the (Spurs), can you f**k"

> "What's it like to see a crowd?"

> "Can you see the (Barnsley) scum? No-o, no-o,
> Can you see the (Barnsley) scum? No-o, no-o,
> Can you see the (Barnsley) scum?
> We can't see a f**king one,
> Woah-oh, oh, oh, oh, oh, oh, oh!"

> "Where were you at (Gresty Road)?"

> "Are you going to (London Road)? are you f**k!"

This last one is sung, usually, when a large contingent have travelled away to see their team, implying that their counterparts will not turn up in as great a number for the return fixture. Should sufficient numbers of opposing fans turn up to warrant threatening, any number of the following may be used......

"You're gonna get your f**king heads kicked in!"

"You're going home in a (Scunthorpe) ambulance."

"We'll see you all outside."

"You'll never make the station."

"You're just a bunch of w**kers."

"Come and have a go if you think you're hard enough."

Should two numerically and vocally evenly matched followings come across each other, they will almost inevitably trade insults throughout the course of the match - some of which reflect the changes in the scoreline...

"Who the f**king hell are you?"

"You're so sh*t it's unbeleivable."

"You're the sh*t of (Sheffield)."

"If you all hate (Stockport), clap your hands."

"You've come all this way, just to lose."

(In derby games) "You're the worst team in (London)."

"So f**king easy, oh this is so f**king easy."

"We thought you were sh*t, we were right."

"Let's all laugh at (Leicester), let's all laugh at (Leicester),
 Ha, ha, ha, ha,  SH*T!"

"You're going down with the (Bournemouth)."

"We only hate (Bristol City), hate (Bristol City)."

"What's it like to be outclassed?"

"Sh*t on the (City), sh*t on the (City) tonight."

"It's nice to know you're here, it's nice to know you're hear, it's nice to know
 you're here - NOW F**K OFF!"

"Sing when you're winning, you only sing when you're winning."

More specifically, there are several "celebratory" songs which are performed when things are going well, either to further encourage the team, add to the now already boisterous atmosphere or remind the luckless oppostition fans of their dire predicament....

"We're going to win the cup, we're going to win the cup,
And now you're gonna beleive us (x 3!) we're gonna win the cup."

"We shall not, we shall not be moved,
We shall not, we shall not be moved,
'cos we're the team that's gonna win the Football League."

"Here we go again, bobbing up and down like this."

"Let's go f**king mental, let's go f**king mental, La, la, la, la, OOOOH!"

"We're gonna Wembley, we're gonna Wembley, you're not!"

"Wembley, Wembley, we're the famous (Stoke City),
And we're goin' to Wembley."

"Are the (Brentford) going to Wembley? are they f**k!"

"No (Scouse) at Wembley, there won't be no (Scouse) at Wembley."

"You're gonna win f**k all, so what's new?"

"We'll be running round Wembley with the cup, pissed up,
We'll be running round Wembley with the cup, pissed up,
We'll be running round Wembley, running round Wembley...."

"Sing your hearts out for the lads."

.....and so it goes on, and on, and on! There are hundreds more short chants to fit any even vaguely football related topic you can think of, from those intended to abuse specific players ("You bald b**tard, you bald b**tard"), to encouraging exhibitionism amongst any young ladies unfortunate enough to be in attendance ("Get your tits out for the lads!") to the cartload of chants aimed either at the match officials or players of the opposing side who commit any of a wide range of heinous crimes (such as scoring or hacking someone down with a reckless challenge). Unpopular players' returning to a club from which they have recently been transferred, the police, stewards, commentators, managers and ball boys all have their own selection of chants from which they can expect to be either vilified or idolised, and it is this massive variety of emotion-conveying verbal invention which has given rise to so much of the flavour and vibrancy to the British game over the years. Chants are constantly evolving - hardly a game goes by without at least one group of spectators (however small) thinking up a new one to suit a particular circumstance. It is this constant updating which precludes a completely comprehensive catalogue of songs, and so with that sadly inadequate excuse for our having omitted your own particular favourite, that's it - end of book!